GW01337149

Original Title: Strange But True Facts Bodybuilding and Fitness.

© Strange But True Facts Bodybuilding and Fitness, Carlos Martínez Cerdá and Víctor Martínez Cerdá, 2024.

Authors: Víctor Martínez Cerdá and Carlos Martínez Cerdá (V&C Brothers).

© Cover and Illustrations: V&C Brothers.

Layout and Design: V&C Brothers.

All rights reserved.

This publication may not be reproduced, stored, recorded, or transmitted in whole or in part by any means, whether mechanical, photo-chemical, electronic, magnetic, electro-optical, or by photocopying or information retrieval systems, or any other means now known or hereafter invented, without the prior written permission of the copyright holders.

STRANGE BUT TRUE FACTS BODYBUILDING AND FITNESS

1

Eugen Sandow (Friederich Wilhelm Müller: Königsberg, now Kaliningrad, April 2, 1867 - London, October 14, 1925) was a Prussian-born athlete.

Eugen Sandow is considered the father of modern bodybuilding, being the first to perform muscle exhibitions.

Sandow began his career as a circus performer, showcasing his strength and physical abilities in traveling shows across Europe.

However, his passion for musculature and the aesthetics of the human body led him to focus more on developing and exhibiting his muscles.

Throughout his life, Sandow stood out not only for his impressive physique but also for his marketing and self-promotion skills.

He published several books and magazines on physical development and health and developed his own exercise system, which included a series of weights and devices designed to improve musculature.

These methods became the foundation of many modern training programs.

In 1891, Sandow moved to London, where his fame grew rapidly.

It was here that he organized the first modern bodybuilding competition in 1901, known as "The Great Competition."

This event was held at the Royal Albert Hall and attracted a considerable crowd, marking a milestone in the history of bodybuilding.

The winners of this competition received bronze statuettes based on Sandow's own figure.

In addition to his contributions to bodybuilding, Sandow was a visionary in terms of health and wellness.

He advocated for a balanced diet, regular exercise, and a healthy lifestyle at a time when these concepts were not widely known.

His influence endures today, and his name remains synonymous with physical strength and muscular perfection.

Sandow also had an impact on popular culture and entertainment.

His exhibitions were not only displays of strength but also visual spectacles, where he posed on stages designed to highlight his musculature under proper lighting.

This attracted a wide variety of spectators and helped popularize bodybuilding as an art form.

The legacy of Eugen Sandow is broad and enduring.

He not only laid the foundations of modern bodybuilding but also inspired generations of athletes and fitness enthusiasts to pursue physical development and holistic health.

His focus on the aesthetics and functionality of the human body remains a fundamental pillar in contemporary physical training.

Sandow passed away on October 14, 1925, in London, but his influence endures, and his figure remains an iconic reference in the world of bodybuilding and physical health.

2

Ronald Dean Coleman, known as "The King", is widely regarded as one of the greatest bodybuilders in history.

He was born on May 13, 1964, in Monroe, Louisiana, United States.

Coleman excelled in professional bodybuilding by achieving the record for the most victories in International Federation of Bodybuilding & Fitness (IFBB) competitions, with a total of 26 titles.

His impressive career includes eight consecutive victories in the prestigious Mr. Olympia contest, from 1998 to 2005, a record he shares with Lee Haney.

Ronnie Coleman is known for his massive size, symmetry, and exceptional muscle definition.

His training regimen is legendary, characterized by his focus on lifting extremely heavy weights, which allowed him to develop extraordinary musculature.

Coleman trained with an intensity and dedication that inspired numerous bodybuilders and fitness enthusiasts around the world.

Throughout his career, Coleman earned the nickname "The King" due to his absolute dominance on the bodybuilding stage.

His physique and achievements made him an iconic figure in the sport.

In addition to his victories in Mr. Olympia, Coleman also won other important titles, such as the Arnold Classic.

Since retiring from professional competitions, Ronnie Coleman has remained active in the bodybuilding community.

Currently, he is dedicated to giving exhibitions and seminars around the world, sharing his knowledge and experience with new generations of bodybuilders and fitness enthusiasts.

His charisma and humility have made him very beloved and respected in the bodybuilding realm.

Despite having undergone multiple surgeries on his spine and hips due to injuries accumulated throughout his career, Coleman remains a symbol of perseverance and dedication.

3

One of the most significant forces behind the popularization of bodybuilding was specialized publications.

Magazines like "Strength & Health" and "Iron Man", launched in the 1930s and 1940s respectively, offered bodybuilding enthusiasts a window into the world of muscle building.

These publications provided training tips, nutrition advice, and profiles of notable competitors, helping to educate and inspire readers interested in improving their physiques.

"Strength & Health" was founded by Bob Hoffman, who was also known as the "Father of American Weightlifting."

This magazine focused on strength development and overall health, promoting weightlifting and bodybuilding as beneficial activities for everyone.

On the other hand, "Iron Man," created by Peary Rader, also played a crucial role by offering detailed content on training techniques and personal stories from bodybuilders.

However, the emergence of "Muscle & Fitness" under the direction of Joe Weider in 1936 marked a real turning point in the popularization of bodybuilding.

Joe Weider, along with his brother Ben, was a central figure in the development of bodybuilding as both a sport and a lifestyle.

Weider not only founded "Muscle & Fitness" but also other influential magazines like "Flex" and "Shape", creating a media empire that promoted bodybuilding worldwide.

"Muscle & Fitness" offered not only technical and scientific information on training and nutrition but also promoted bodybuilding as a healthy and aspirational lifestyle.

The magazine included articles on exercise routines, diets, supplements, and profiles of famous bodybuilders, as well as practical advice for achieving physical goals.

The impact of these publications was enormous.

They helped create a global community of bodybuilding enthusiasts, provided a platform for professional bodybuilders to share their knowledge and experiences, and elevated the profile of bodybuilding within the fitness and health industry.

Moreover, these magazines served as vehicles for bodybuilding competitions, promoting events and highlighting winners, which contributed to the growing popularity and legitimacy of the sport.

4

Iconic figures like Steve Reeves (1926-2000), who won the Mr. America title in 1947 and later became a movie star, played a crucial role in bringing bodybuilding to the general public.

Reeves, with his sculpted physique and success in film, demonstrated that bodybuilding could be a gateway to success in other areas, inspiring future generations to follow in his footsteps.

Steve Reeves was born on January 21, 1926, in Glasgow, Montana, and became interested in bodybuilding at a young age.

His dedication to training and his exceptional genetics led him to win several important titles, including Mr. America in 1947, Mr. World in 1948, and Mr. Universe in 1950.

These achievements gave him significant visibility and opened doors to opportunities beyond competitive bodybuilding.

Reeves' physique, characterized by its symmetry, classic proportions, and aesthetics, made him the ideal of male musculature of his time.

His success in bodybuilding competitions was just the beginning of a broader career.

Reeves leveraged his impressive physique and charisma to venture into cinema, where he achieved notable fame.

In the 1950s, Reeves moved to Italy, where he became a star of peplum cinema, a genre of epic films set in classical antiquity.

His most famous role was Hercules in "Hercules" (1958) and its sequel "Hercules Unchained" (1959).

These films were major hits and helped popularize bodybuilding by showcasing a muscular physique on the big screen, something that was uncommon at the time.

Reeves' success in cinema had a significant impact on the public perception of bodybuilding.

He demonstrated that a well-developed physique could open doors in the entertainment industry and beyond.

His charisma, on-screen presence, and acting skills, combined with his impressive physique, inspired many young people to pursue physical training, hoping to emulate his success.

Moreover, Reeves promoted a balanced and healthy approach to bodybuilding, emphasizing the importance of symmetry and aesthetics over sheer muscle size.

His legacy in bodybuilding endures today, not only as an icon of the golden age of bodybuilding but also as a role model for those seeking to combine musculature with grace and elegance.

Steve Reeves passed away on May 1, 2000, but his influence remains.

5

The first official bodybuilding competition was "The Great Competition", held in 1901 and organized by Eugen Sandow.

This event marked a significant milestone in the history of bodybuilding, setting a precedent for future competitions.

Sandow, known as the father of modern bodybuilding, sought to promote musculature and the aesthetics of the human body through this competition.

"The Great Competition" took place at the Royal Albert Hall in London and attracted over 2,000 spectators, a remarkable attendance for the time.

The prizes awarded in this competition included bronze statues representing Sandow in classic bodybuilding poses, as well as medals for the winners.

These prizes symbolized excellence in musculature and physical symmetry, fundamental values in bodybuilding.

The organization and success of "The Great Competition" not only validated bodybuilding as a legitimate sport but also helped establish the standards and criteria still used in modern competitions.

The influence of Sandow and the impact of this event were crucial for the growth and popularization of bodybuilding worldwide.

6

The formation of bodybuilding federations and the organization of more structured competitions were key steps in the evolution of the sport.

The Amateur Athletic Association (AAA) and the International Federation of Bodybuilding & Fitness (IFBB) played crucial roles in this development, providing an organizational framework and standardized rules for competitions.

The IFBB, founded by brothers Joe and Ben Weider in 1946, became one of the most influential organizations in bodybuilding.

This federation promoted the sport globally and created the Mr. Olympia contest in 1965, which quickly became the most prestigious bodybuilding competition in the world.

The creation of the Mr. Olympia competition in 1965 was a crucial step in the development of competitive bodybuilding.

Designed by Joe Weider to be the pinnacle of bodybuilding competitions, Mr. Olympia brought together the best athletes from around the world, creating a stage where they could compete for the title of "The Best Bodybuilder in the World."

This competition not only raised the standard of excellence within the sport but also attracted media and public attention, increasing the visibility and popularity of bodybuilding.

Over time, bodybuilding saw the development of a number of other federations and competitions, each with its own rules, categories, and philosophies.

Some of these federations focused on natural bodybuilding, imposing strict anti-doping policies to ensure that athletes competed without the use of prohibited substances.

Among these federations, the National Amateur Bodybuilders Association (NABBA) and the International Natural Bodybuilding Association (INBA/PNBA) stand out for their commitment to maintaining the integrity of the sport through rigorous drug testing and the promotion of fair and equitable competition.

The existence of multiple federations and competitions has allowed bodybuilding to evolve and diversify, offering opportunities for a wider variety of athletes and competition styles.

7

The "Golden Era of Bodybuilding" primarily spans the years from the late 60s to the late 70s, a period characterized by unprecedented growth in the popularity of bodybuilding and the emergence of some of the sport's most iconic figures.

During this time, bodybuilding underwent a cultural and aesthetic transformation, driven by changes in ideals of male physique, innovations in training and nutrition, and increased media visibility.

Arnold Schwarzenegger, Franco Columbu, Frank Zane, Lou Ferrigno, and Sergio Oliva are just a few of the names that dominated the bodybuilding scene during this era.

These athletes stood out not only for their impressive physiques but also for their charisma and ability to connect with the public.

Schwarzenegger, in particular, became the face of bodybuilding worldwide, winning the Mr. Olympia title seven times and using his fame in the sport as a springboard to a successful career in film and eventually politics.

This golden era is also distinguished by a shift in the aesthetic ideals of bodybuilding.

While previous decades emphasized muscle mass, bodybuilders of this era strived for a more balanced and symmetrical physique, with great attention to muscle definition and proportion.

This ideal is reflected in the figure of Frank Zane, known for his aesthetically pleasing and highly symmetrical physique, which allowed him to win three Mr. Olympia titles despite competing at a significantly lower weight than many of his rivals.

The "Golden Era of Bodybuilding" was driven by the growing popularity of gyms and increased media coverage, including the influence of the documentary "Pumping Iron" (1977), which introduced Schwarzenegger and other bodybuilders to a broader audience, helping to demystify and popularize the sport.

After the close of the so-called "Golden Era of Bodybuilding" in the late 70s and early 80s, bodybuilding entered a new phase of evolution and growth.

This new era was marked by the emergence of athletes who took the sport to new levels of muscle mass and professionalism, as well as changes in fitness culture and public perception of bodybuilding.

The transition towards greater muscle mass and the use of advanced training techniques and supplementation became the norm, influencing future generations of bodybuilders and fitness enthusiasts worldwide.

8

The "Era of Giants" in bodybuilding encompasses the 1990s and the early 21st century, a period characterized by competitors who took muscle size to unprecedented levels.

This period is marked by iconic figures like Dorian Yates and Ronnie Coleman, who redefined the standards of the sport.

Dorian Yates, known as "The Shadow," dominated the Mr. Olympia competition with six consecutive victories from 1992 to 1997.

Yates introduced a high-intensity training approach known as "Heavy Duty," which emphasized short, extremely heavy sets.

His massive physique, combined with surprising definition and symmetry, marked the beginning of a new era in bodybuilding, where extreme size became the norm.

Ronnie Coleman, on the other hand, is one of the most dominant figures in bodybuilding history.

He won the Mr. Olympia title eight consecutive times from 1998 to 2005, matching Lee Haney's record.

Coleman was known for his incredibly rigorous work ethic and for lifting weights that pushed the limits of what was possible, making him a legend both on and off the stage.

His training routines, which included extremely heavy lifts, are legendary and have inspired countless bodybuilders.

The "Era of Giants" was characterized not only by the presence of Yates and Coleman but also by the emergence of Jay Cutler, another icon of modern bodybuilding.

Cutler emerged as a central figure during and after Coleman's era.

Known for his determination and methodical approach to training and nutrition, Cutler won the Mr. Olympia title four times (2006, 2007, 2009, and 2010).

The rivalry between Coleman and Cutler was one of the most exciting duels in bodybuilding history, attracting legions of fans and elevating the sport's profile.

Cutler is admired not only for his competitive achievements but also for his ability to stay at the top of the sport for many years.

His scientific and detailed approach to bodybuilding, along with his charismatic presence, has left a lasting mark on the sport.

During this era, bodybuilding became even more professionalized, with competitors focusing intensely on nutrition, supplementation, and advanced training strategies.

The use of technology and sports science also became more deeply integrated into athletes' routines, allowing for continuous improvements in performance and physical development.

9

As bodybuilding advanced into the 21st century, the sport saw greater diversification with the introduction of new categories such as Men's Physique, Classic Physique, and Bikini, adapting to a wider range of physical ideals and attracting a more varied audience.

This diversification allowed more people to identify with the sport and feel motivated to participate, as the new categories value aesthetics, proportion, and symmetry over sheer muscle mass.

Chris Bumstead has become the face of Classic Physique and modern bodybuilding in general.

He has won the Mr. Olympia Classic Physique title multiple times, establishing himself as a role model for millions of teenagers and enthusiasts worldwide.

Bumstead is known for his Golden Era aesthetics, emphasizing symmetry, proportion, and a classic look reminiscent of the great bodybuilders of the past.

His focus and dedication have deeply resonated within the fitness community, earning him a loyal and passionate fan base.

The digital era has transformed how bodybuilders interact with their followers, share their training and nutrition routines, and promote the sport.

Social media has allowed athletes like Ronnie Coleman, Jay Cutler, Ramon Dino, and Chris Bumstead to build global communities.

Platforms like Instagram, YouTube, and TikTok have democratized access to information about bodybuilding, allowing training tips, diets, and motivation to reach people from all over the world, inspiring many to pursue their own fitness goals.

From the end of the Golden Era to the present day, bodybuilding has continued to evolve, embracing new technologies, training techniques, and nutritional trends, while maintaining the spirit of personal improvement and physical excellence that has defined the sport since its inception.

The incorporation of advanced technologies in training, such as fitness apps and health monitoring devices, has allowed bodybuilders to optimize their routines and significantly improve their performance.

Key figures like Eugen Sandow, Joe Weider, Arnold Schwarzenegger, Lee Haney, Dorian Yates, Ronnie Coleman, Jay Cutler, and Chris Bumstead have left their mark on bodybuilding history not only for their impressive physiques but also for their ability to inspire and lead within the bodybuilding community.

10

A high-protein diet destroys your kidneys: FALSE.

Protein, after being hydrolyzed and filtered into the bloodstream in the form of amino acids, performs essential structural and regulatory functions for the body.

Excessive restriction of its intake can result in these functions not being satisfied, especially if there is a deficiency of EAAs (essential amino acids not synthesized by the body).

Excess amino acids are filtered by the kidneys through a degradation process that the body uses to balance the anabolic and catabolic metabolism of amino acids since they cannot be stored.

Amino acids can be degraded by transamination and/or oxidative deamination.

It was hypothesized that subjecting the kidney to the detoxification process of ammonia produced by oxidative deamination in the urea cycle increased glomerular pressure and hyperfiltration.

However, despite this theoretical logic, there is no evidence that high protein intake causes kidney damage in healthy individuals.

Studies have not shown a significant correlation between a high-protein diet and kidney damage in individuals with healthy kidneys.

It is important to note that this conclusion applies to people without pre-existing kidney disease.

To ensure that protein intake is not excessive and does not pose a risk to kidney function, it is sufficient to periodically measure urea, creatinine, blood urea nitrogen, and glomerular filtration rate.

These tests are useful tools for monitoring kidney health and adjusting protein intake if necessary.

11

Creatine can make you retain water: FALSE.

Creatine is a nitrogenous organic acid with strong evidence supporting its effectiveness and is widely used by athletes.

Chronic consumption of creatine saturates the free creatine stores within myocytes, favoring the synthesis of phosphocreatine through the phosphorylation of available free molecules, thereby increasing our capacity to sustain anaerobic efforts.

Creatine consumption is associated with weight gain caused by an increase in total body water.

However, while it is true that creatine consumption increases water concentrations, this increase occurs within muscle cells.

This phenomenon does not imply subcutaneous water retention, which is generally associated with a "bloated" appearance or water retention in other contexts.

As shown by Powers et al. (2003), "fluid distribution did not change."

This means that creatine does not cause a redistribution of body water to extracellular spaces but rather increases the volume of water within muscle cells.

This intracellular increase is beneficial, as it can improve cellular hydration and contribute to better muscle performance and recovery.

Therefore, the myth that creatine causes undesirable water retention is incorrect.

In reality, creatine contributes to an increase in muscle mass and strength without the negative effects associated with extracellular water retention.

12

Salt retains fluids: FALSE.

Salt has the capacity to retain fluids primarily when there are significant variations in its consumption.

These abrupt changes in salt intake can alter the osmolarity of the extracellular and intracellular environment, which in turn inhibits the secretion of aldosterone, a hormone responsible for sodium reabsorption and maintaining osmotic pressure.

When aldosterone is inhibited, the body reduces fluid loss to maintain and increase fluid volume, thus seeking to reduce the osmolarity of the environment through a sodium dilution mechanism.

This process can lead to temporary fluid retention until the body adapts to the new levels of salt consumption.

With a stable sodium intake, regardless of whether it is higher or lower, osmolarity does not undergo significant variations.

In this context, aldosterone is secreted in stable amounts, which does not produce variations in fluid volume.

Thus, the body maintains an adequate fluid balance without excessive fluid retention.

In summary, fluid retention due to salt is a transient phenomenon that occurs mainly with abrupt changes in sodium intake.

With consistent consumption, the body efficiently regulates fluid and sodium levels, avoiding unnecessary retention.

13

Carbohydrates are the culprit of weight gain and/or lack of fat loss: FALSE.

The true culprit of weight gain is a positive energy balance, that is, a hypercaloric diet where calorie intake exceeds energy expenditure.

Insulin, whose production is stimulated by the consumption of large amounts of carbohydrates, can acutely inhibit lipolysis, that is, it can reduce the breakdown of fats; however, this effect is not significant in the overall context of weight loss.

Studies like Hu et al. (2012) demonstrate that when a group of people is subjected to a weight loss program with isocaloric diets (the same number of calories) but with different macronutrient compositions (low fat vs. low carbohydrate), the results may vary slightly but follow a general trend of weight loss.

In this study, a weight loss of -0.9 kg was observed in the low-fat diet group and -2.0 kg in the low-carbohydrate diet group.

The source of the consumed energy is less relevant as long as the daily energy balance is positive or negative.

In other words, for weight loss, what is crucial is maintaining a calorie deficit, regardless of whether the calories come from carbohydrates, fats, or proteins.

Therefore, blaming carbohydrates exclusively for weight gain is incorrect and oversimplifies the complex energy and metabolic balance of the human body.

14

You only gain muscle mass between 6 and 12 repetitions: FALSE.

The repetition range is irrelevant when the volume is equalized.

The most important factor for producing muscle mass gains is working in a repetition range between 8 and 35 repetitions with a high level of effort (close to muscle failure).

Studies by Brad Schoenfeld and other researchers have shown that, after 8 weeks of training, there are no significant differences in muscle mass gain between groups that performed high repetitions (25-35RM) and low repetitions (8-12RM), as long as both groups trained with maximum volitional effort, i.e., close to muscle failure.

This suggests that as long as an adequate level of effort and training volume is maintained, significant muscle gains can be achieved across a wide range of repetitions.

The total training volume (sets x repetitions x load) and effort close to failure are critical factors for muscle hypertrophy.

Variability in the repetition range allows individuals to tailor their workouts to their personal preferences and abilities without compromising muscle gains.

This flexible approach can help prevent boredom and excessive fatigue and can be more sustainable in the long term.

15

Post-workout is the best time to take protein: FALSE.

The most important factor for promoting MPS (muscle protein synthesis) is maintaining a continuous state of aminoacidemia throughout the day.

Consuming protein peri-workout (before, during, or after exercise) can have metabolic benefits compared to consuming it at another time of the day; however, the need to consume protein post-workout depends on its consumption pre- and intra-workout.

In a study conducted by Schoenfeld and Aragon in 2017, it was shown that consuming 25 grams of whey protein before or after training did not present significant differences in the body composition of the experimental subjects throughout the entire intervention.

This suggests that the specific timing of protein intake is not as crucial as meeting the total daily intake and maintaining an appropriate distribution throughout the day.

To maximize muscle protein synthesis, protein intake should be sufficient and properly distributed.

According to Schoenfeld and Aragon (2018), consuming 0.40 to 0.55 grams of protein per kilogram of body weight in four meals a day is sufficient to maximize MPS.

This strategy ensures that the body has a constant supply of the amino acids necessary for muscle repair and growth.

16

**More repetitions with less weight for definition:
HALF FALSE.**

The belief that during periods of body fat loss you should reduce the load and increase the number of repetitions stems from the idea that longer exercise results in greater energy expenditure, to such an extent that it becomes a relevant factor to control.

This is not entirely false, as there are studies showing that depending on the energetic characteristics of the exercise performed, the energy expenditure can vary from ≈3 to 30 kcal·min−1, potentially reaching 40 kcal·min−1 in exercises involving large amounts of muscle mass (Reis et al. 2011).

The energy expenditure of a free, multi-joint, dynamic exercise like lunges is not the same as a static, single-joint exercise like a bicep curl.

However, the main determinant of fat loss is the energy balance.

Therefore, the number of repetitions performed is actually a minor factor in this process.

Given that muscle mass gains are similar between exercises with more and less load (more and fewer repetitions) as long as the effort level is close to maximum volition, it might be interesting to include exercises that involve a large amount of muscle mass with higher repetition ranges to induce greater energy expenditure.

On the other hand, in single-joint exercises where the amount of muscle mass involved is smaller, the difference in energy expenditure between a set of 8RM and 30RM is negligible.

Let's not forget that this is a minor factor in the fat loss process, emphasizing the calorie factor as more important.

17

"NO PAIN, NO GAIN," or more is always better: FALSE.

Training volume follows a Gaussian bell curve in terms of effectiveness.

It is necessary to reach a minimum threshold of work for the stimulus to be sufficient to generate adaptations.

However, excessive volume can be counterproductive if it exceeds the recovery capacity, negatively affecting future training sessions by reducing the tonnage and/or frequency.

Regarding intensity, to maximize hypertrophy and muscle mass gain, the most effective sets are those performed close to muscle failure.

Training with a high effort level is crucial for generating significant muscular adaptations.

It is important to find an appropriate balance in training volume and intensity.

An excessive focus on volume without considering recovery capacity can lead to overtraining and a decrease in performance.

Likewise, insufficient intensity can result in inadequate stimuli for muscle growth.

Ultimately, it is essential to gradually increase the quantity and quality of work to continue producing adaptations.

This involves not only increasing volume and intensity but also optimizing training programming and ensuring that the body has enough time to recover and adapt to the stimuli.

18

Famous quotes from bodybuilders.

1. Arnold Schwarzenegger:
- "The worst thing I can be is the same as everybody else. I hate that."
- "You can't climb the ladder of success with your hands in your pockets."
- "The mind is the limit. As long as the mind can envision the fact that you can do something, you can do it, as long as you really believe 100%."
- "The resistance that you fight physically in the gym and the resistance that you fight in life can only build a strong character."
- "Failure is not an option. Everyone can succeed."

2. Ronnie Coleman:
- "Yeah, buddy!"
- "Ain't nothing but a peanut."
- "Everybody wants to be a bodybuilder, but nobody wants to lift heavy weights."
- "My daily routine is to train like it's the last day I'll ever train."
- "Hard work and dedication are the keys to success."

3. Lee Haney:
- "Train to stimulate, not annihilate."
- "Exercise to stimulate, not annihilate. The world wasn't formed in a day, and neither were we. Set small goals and build upon them."

4. Dorian Yates:
- "Nothing tastes as good as being shredded feels."
- "Your mind is the strongest and most valuable muscle you can grow in the gym."
- "Suffering in training translates to success in competition."
- "The real pain is the satisfaction of knowing you've given everything you have."

5. Frank Zane:
- "Live your life with a code of ethics, maintain your integrity at all times. That is the only way to achieve your goals."

6. Jay Cutler:
- "Success comes from the ability to see the vision and follow through with it."
- "There is no secret routine. There are no secrets. What we have is hard work."

7. Phil Heath:
- "I may not be the biggest, I may not be the strongest, but I sure am the toughest!"
- "If you don't challenge yourself, you will never realize what you can become."

8. Rich Piana:
- "Whatever it takes."

9. Kai Greene:
- "The mind is everything. If you don't believe you can do something, then you can't."
- "Bodybuilding is like any other sport. To be successful, you must dedicate yourself 100% to your training, diet, and mental approach."

10. Lou Ferrigno:
- "To me, life is being continuously hungry. The meaning of life is not simply to exist, to survive, but to move ahead, to go up, to achieve, to conquer."
- "Success is the process of continually striving to become better."

11. Flex Wheeler:
- "Pain is temporary. It may last a minute, an hour, a day, or a year, but eventually it will subside and something else will take its place. If I quit, however, it lasts forever."

12. Rich Gaspari:
- "Hard work is the best way to achieve your dreams. There are no shortcuts."

13. Sergio Oliva:
- "The only way to win is to outwork your competitors."
- "You have to focus on your goals and work constantly to achieve them."
- "Legacy is built not just with victories, but with daily work and passion for the sport."

14. Tom Platz:
- "Training is not just about the physical. It is therapy for the soul."
- "For me, lifting weights is the same love I have for life itself."
- "The key to success is to continue growing in all areas of life: mentally, emotionally, spiritually, as well as physically."

15. Franco Columbu:
- "Discipline and consistency are the foundation of success."
- "Always strive to be the best version of yourself, both physically and mentally."

16. Jay Cutler:
- "Never underestimate the power of believing in yourself."
- "It's not just about winning. It's about improving every day and never giving up."

17. Dexter Jackson:
- "Age is just a number. You can achieve anything if you set your mind to it and work hard."

18. Kevin Levrone:
- "It's not about how much you can lift, but how much you can endure and keep moving forward."

19. Branch Warren:
- "Pain is weakness leaving the body."

20. Larry Scott:
- "Bodybuilding is a marathon, not a sprint. It's about long-term commitment."

21. Shawn Ray:
- "Success is not a destination, it's a continuous journey of improvement and dedication."

22. Markus Rühl:
- "Strength does not come from physical capacity. It comes from an indomitable will."

23. Lee Labrada:
- "Perfection is not attainable, but if we chase perfection we can achieve excellence."

24. Frank McGrath:
- "Pain is just weakness leaving the body."

25. Robby Robinson:
- "Bodybuilding is like any other sport. To succeed, you must dedicate yourself 100% to your training, diet, and mental approach."

26. Samir Bannout:
- "The secret to success is to never stop trying."

27. Dennis Wolf:
- "It's not about being the best. It's about being better than you were yesterday."

28. Roelly Winklaar:
- "True success comes from the passion for what you do and the dedication to being the best at it."

19

The origins of bodybuilding in ancient Greece and Rome can be traced through cultural practices and values that exalted physical strength, musculature, and athletic performance.

These civilizations greatly valued the perfection of the human body, both for aesthetic and functional reasons.

In Ancient Greece, the cult of the body and physical preparation were fundamental aspects of the culture.

The Greeks believed that a strong and well-developed body was a manifestation of personal excellence (areté) and the harmony between mind and body.

This idea was reflected in myths and heroic figures, such as Hercules, who represented the ideal of the strong and virtuous man.

The Olympic Games, which began in 776 BC, were one of the main platforms where athletes demonstrated their strength and physical abilities.

Greek athletes trained in gymnasiums, where they performed resistance exercises, weightlifting, and other intensive physical training.

The concept of the gymnasium (from the Greek "gymnós", meaning naked) was deeply rooted in Greek culture, as athletes competed naked to show the purity and perfection of their bodies.

Weight training was a common practice among Greek athletes.

They used tools like halteres (weights similar to modern dumbbells) to improve their strength and musculature.

Halteres were used for both lifting and jumping exercises, highlighting the importance of endurance and power in their physical preparation.

In Ancient Rome, the admiration for strength and musculature was also evident, although with some cultural differences.

The Romans adopted many Greek athletic practices but also developed their own forms of physical training.

Gladiators, for example, were intensely trained for fights in the arena, which involved a rigorous regime of exercises and weightlifting.

The Romans built large training facilities known as ludus, where gladiators and other athletes prepared themselves.

Physical training in Rome was not only a matter of competition but also of military preparation.

Roman soldiers followed physical training programs to stay fit and ready for battle.

Besides gladiators and soldiers, Roman citizens also engaged in physical exercises at the thermae, which were public bath complexes that included gymnasiums.

Here, Romans participated in various physical activities, from weightlifting to wrestling and running.

20

Superstitions and Rituals.

1. Arnold Schwarzenegger: Although no specific superstition is known, Arnold had very strict rituals and routines before each competition. For example, he was known for visualizing his poses and routines in great detail, firmly believing in the power of visualization to enhance his performance.

2. Ronnie Coleman: He always carried a cross with him before each competition as a way to seek protection and luck at his events. Additionally, he had an extremely rigorous training routine that he followed religiously, believing that any deviation could affect his performance.

3. Jay Cutler: He was known for having specific preparation rituals before each competition, such as eating the same foods and following a strict daily routine. He believed that consistency in his preparation gave him a psychological and physical advantage.

4. Dorian Yates: He often had a very mental approach to his training and competitions. He believed in the importance of concentration and a positive mindset. His methodical and almost ritualistic approach to his preparation was a way to ensure his success.

5. Phil Heath: He has a strong belief in the power of mentality and mental preparation. Before competitions, he dedicates time to meditation and visualization, ensuring that his mind is as prepared as his body.

6. Kai Greene: He is known for his almost philosophical approach to bodybuilding. He often talks about the mind-body connection and the importance of meditation and visualization. Although he doesn't have traditional superstitions, his preparation includes mental and emotional rituals that he considers crucial to his success.

21

Fixes in Bodybuilding Competitions.

1. Arnold Schwarzenegger and Mr. Olympia 1980:
The 1980 Mr. Olympia is one of the most controversial contests in bodybuilding history. Arnold Schwarzenegger decided to participate in the event after a five-year retirement and won the title, despite many believing he was not in his best form. Schwarzenegger's victory was met with boos and criticism, and several competitors, including Mike Mentzer, claimed the result had been manipulated in Arnold's favor due to his influence and status in the sport.

2. Joe Weider and the IFBB:
Joe Weider, co-founder of the IFBB (International Federation of Bodybuilding & Fitness) and creator of Mr. Olympia, has been accused of having undue influence over competition results. Some bodybuilders and critics have suggested that Weider favored certain competitors who were under contract with his supplement companies or who regularly appeared in his magazines.

3. Ronnie Coleman and Mr. Olympia:
During Ronnie Coleman's reign as Mr. Olympia (1998-2005), there were rumors and accusations that the results were fixed in his favor. Despite his undisputed dominance and impressive physique, some critics argued that other competitors deserved to win in certain years but were overlooked due to favoritism towards Coleman.

4. Flex Wheeler and the Arnold Classic:
Flex Wheeler, one of the most aesthetic bodybuilders of the 1990s, was the subject of rumors about fixes at the Arnold Classic. Although he won the title multiple times, there were insinuations that certain results were influenced by his relationship with the event's organizers and sponsors.

5. Phil Heath and Mr. Olympia:
During Phil Heath's winning streak at Mr. Olympia (2011-2017), accusations of favoritism emerged. Some competitors and fans believed that other bodybuilders, like Kai Greene, deserved to win in certain years but were overshadowed by Heath due to his popularity and sponsorship.

6. Competitors withdrawing in protest:
There have been cases where competitors have withdrawn from competitions in protest over what they perceived as unfair decisions. For example, at the 1981 Mr. Olympia, Franco Columbu won the title after returning from a severe injury. His victory was highly criticized, and several competitors, including Roy Callender and Mike Mentzer, withdrew in protest, claiming the result had been fixed.

The most important bodybuilding competitions.

1. Mr. Olympia:
- **Description:** It is the most prestigious bodybuilding competition in the world, organized by the International Federation of Bodybuilding & Fitness (IFBB).
- **Prizes:** In 2023, the winner of Mr. Olympia received a prize of $400,000. The total prize pool for the competition exceeds one million dollars, distributed among various categories and finalists.

2. Arnold Classic:
- **Description:** Founded by Arnold Schwarzenegger and Jim Lorimer, this competition is one of the most recognized and is held annually in Columbus, Ohio.
- **Prizes:** The winner of the Arnold Classic usually receives around $130,000, along with other prizes and trophies. The total prize pool for the event also includes money for the finalists and winners of other categories.

3. IFBB World Bodybuilding Championships:
- **Description:** Organized by the IFBB, it is one of the most important championships at both amateur and professional levels.
- **Prizes:** Although cash prizes vary, winners typically receive international recognition, trophies, and sometimes monetary prizes, especially in professional categories.

4. NPC National Championships:
- **Description:** It is one of the most important amateur competitions in the United States, organized by the National Physique Committee (NPC).
- **Prizes:** Winners get the opportunity to turn professional and compete in IFBB events. The monetary prizes are not as high as in professional competitions, but the value lies in achieving professional status.

5. The New York Pro:
- **Description:** One of the most important professional competitions in the United States, attracting many elite competitors.
- **Prizes:** The prize for the winner is usually around $10,000 to $15,000, with additional prizes for the finalists.

6. The Tampa Pro:
- **Description:** Another important competition on the IFBB calendar, serving as a qualifier for Mr. Olympia.
- **Prizes:** Similar to the New York Pro, prizes are usually in the range of $10,000 to $15,000 for the winner.

7. The Arnold Classic Europe:
- **Description:** Part of the Arnold Sports Festival, this event is held in Europe and is one of the most important outside the United States.
- **Prizes:** Monetary prizes vary, but the main winner receives a significant sum, similar to the Arnold Classic in Ohio, although slightly less.

8. The Dubai Muscle Show:
- **Description:** An event that has gained prominence in recent years, attracting competitors from around the world.
- **Prizes:** The cash prizes are competitive, with several thousand dollars for the winners of the main categories.

These competitions not only offer cash prizes but also recognition, sponsorship, and professional opportunities for bodybuilders.

Monetary prizes can vary each year and depend on the category and level of the competition, but the mentioned events are known for their significant financial incentives and prestige.

23

Countries with the Most Fans.

1. United States:
- **Number of Bodybuilders:** The United States has the largest number of bodybuilders and bodybuilding enthusiasts. It is estimated that there are approximately 700,000 active bodybuilders.
- **Enthusiasts:** Around 50 million people practice some form of weight training and fitness.

2. Brazil:
- **Number of Bodybuilders:** Brazil has a strong fitness and bodybuilding culture, with around 300,000 competitive bodybuilders.
- **Enthusiasts:** It is estimated that 20 million Brazilians regularly practice bodybuilding and fitness.

3. India:
- **Number of Bodybuilders:** India has seen significant growth in the popularity of bodybuilding in recent years, with approximately 200,000 competitive bodybuilders.
- **Enthusiasts:** About 15 million Indians are involved in bodybuilding and fitness.

4. Russia:
- **Number of Bodybuilders:** Russia has a strong tradition in strength sports, including bodybuilding, with around 150,000 active bodybuilders.
- **Enthusiasts:** It is estimated that 10 million Russians participate in weightlifting and fitness activities.

5. Germany:
- **Number of Bodybuilders:** Germany has a well-established bodybuilding community, with approximately 100,000 competitive bodybuilders.
- **Enthusiasts:** Around 8 million Germans practice bodybuilding and fitness.

6. United Kingdom:
- **Number of Bodybuilders:** The United Kingdom has an active bodybuilding community, with around 80,000 competitors.
- **Enthusiasts:** Approximately 10 million people in the UK participate in some form of weight training.

7. Australia:
- **Number of Bodybuilders:** Australia has a vibrant bodybuilding community with about 70,000 competitive bodybuilders.
- **Enthusiasts:** Approximately 6 million Australians are involved in fitness and bodybuilding.

8. Canada:
- Number of Bodybuilders: Canada has an active bodybuilding community with around 60,000 competitive bodybuilders.
- Enthusiasts: Approximately 7 million Canadians participate in bodybuilding and fitness.

9. Mexico:
- **Number of Bodybuilders:** Mexico has a growing bodybuilding community, with approximately 50,000 competitive bodybuilders.
- **Enthusiasts:** About 5 million Mexicans are involved in fitness and bodybuilding activities.

10. Japan:
- **Number of Bodybuilders:** Japan has seen an increase in the popularity of bodybuilding, with around 40,000 competitive bodybuilders.
- **Enthusiasts:** Approximately 4 million Japanese participate in fitness and weightlifting.

24

Notable Bodybuilding Movies.

1. Pumping Iron (1977):
- **Description:** This documentary is probably the most famous movie about bodybuilding. Directed by George Butler and Robert Fiore, it follows several bodybuilders as they prepare for the 1975 Mr. Olympia competition.
- **Stars:** Arnold Schwarzenegger, Lou Ferrigno, Franco Columbu.
- **Impact:** "Pumping Iron" catapulted Arnold Schwarzenegger to international fame and helped popularize bodybuilding in the mainstream. The film showcased the dedication and effort required to compete at the highest level and helped change the public perception of bodybuilding.

2. Stay Hungry (1976):
- **Description:** A comedy-drama directed by Bob Rafelson, based on the novel by Charles Gaines. The story centers on a young businessman who becomes involved in the world of bodybuilding.
- Stars: Jeff Bridges, Sally Field, Arnold Schwarzenegger.
- **Impact:** Arnold Schwarzenegger won a Golden Globe for his performance, which solidified his transition from bodybuilder to movie star.

3. The Comeback (1980):
- **Description:** This documentary follows Arnold Schwarzenegger's return to competitive bodybuilding after retirement, focusing on his preparation for the 1980 Mr. Olympia.
- **Stars:** Arnold Schwarzenegger.
- **Impact:** The film provides an intimate look at Arnold's preparation and competitive mindset, though the controversy surrounding his 1980 victory is also reflected.

4. Generation Iron (2013):
- **Description:** A documentary directed by Vlad Yudin considered the spiritual successor to "Pumping Iron." The film follows several modern bodybuilders as they prepare to compete in Mr. Olympia.
- **Stars:** Phil Heath, Kai Greene, Branch Warren, Dennis Wolf.
- **Impact:** "Generation Iron" helped renew interest in contemporary bodybuilding and provided an updated look at the lives and challenges of professional bodybuilders.

5. Bigger (2018):
- **Description:** A biographical film that tells the story of brothers Joe and Ben Weider, who were instrumental in the creation of the IFBB and Mr. Olympia.
- **Stars:** Tyler Hoechlin, Julianne Hough, Kevin Durand, Calum Von Moger (as Arnold Schwarzenegger).
- **Impact:** The film celebrates the achievements of the Weiders and their influence in the bodybuilding world, highlighting their role in popularizing the sport.

6. The Perfect Physique (2015):
- **Description:** A documentary that follows several fitness models and bodybuilders as they compete and try to balance their personal and professional lives.
- **Stars:** Jeremy Buendia, Tavi Castro, Jason Poston.
- **Impact:** The film offers a behind-the-scenes look at the lives of fitness models and bodybuilders, highlighting their challenges and sacrifices.

7. Generation Iron 2 (2017):
- **Description:** The sequel to "Generation Iron" that explores how bodybuilding has evolved with the influence of social media and digital marketing.
- **Stars:** Kai Greene, Calum Von Moger, Rich Piana.
- **Impact:** This film highlights how digital platforms have changed the way bodybuilders promote themselves and connect with their followers.

8. Born to be King (2000):
- **Description:** A documentary that follows Ronnie Coleman on his journey to his third Mr. Olympia title.
- **Stars:** Ronnie Coleman.
- **Impact:** Provides an up-close look at the training routine and life of one of the most dominant bodybuilders in history.

9. The King (2018):
- **Description:** A documentary that celebrates Ronnie Coleman's career, focusing on his victories and the impact of his career on his personal life.
- **Stars:** Ronnie Coleman.
- **Impact:** Offers perspective on the sacrifices and physical consequences of high-level bodybuilding.

10. Generation Iron 3 (2018):
- **Description:** The third installment of the "Generation Iron" series explores the diversity of bodybuilding worldwide, highlighting different styles and approaches to the sport.
- **Stars:** Kai Greene, Hadi Choopan, Brandon Curry.
- **Impact:** The film shows how bodybuilding has evolved globally and how different cultures embrace the sport, offering a broader and more diverse perspective.

11. CT Fletcher: My Magnificent Obsession (2015):
- **Description:** A documentary about the life of CT Fletcher, a bodybuilder and powerlifter who overcame serious health issues to become an inspiring figure in fitness.
- **Stars:** CT Fletcher.
- **Impact:** Showcases resilience and determination, inspiring many in the fitness community.

25

The history of female bodybuilding is a fascinating and relatively recent evolution compared to male bodybuilding.

Although women have participated in physical and athletic activities for centuries, female bodybuilding as a formal sport began to gain popularity in the second half of the 20th century.

In the 1960s and 1970s, physical fitness and fitness culture began to gain popularity among women, focusing more on toning and definition than on extreme muscle development.

One of the pioneers was Lisa Lyon, who won the first women's bodybuilding contest in 1979, breaking gender stereotypes.

The first official women's bodybuilding contest, the U.S. Women's National Physique Championship, was held in 1978, marking the beginning of formal competitions.

In 1980, the IFBB organized the first Ms. Olympia competition, with Rachel McLish as the winner, popularizing female bodybuilding.

As more women began to compete, controversies arose over the aesthetic ideal, with some competitions valuing extreme muscle definition and others preferring a softer appearance.

In the 1990s, the documentary "Pumping Iron II: The Women" helped increase the visibility of the sport.

New categories such as fitness and figure emerged, emphasizing symmetry and presentation.

Lenda Murray became a dominant figure, winning the Ms. Olympia title eight times between 1990 and 1997, and then again in 2002 and 2003.

In the 2000s, new categories were introduced to diversify the sport.

The bikini category was introduced in 2010, designed for women seeking an athletic and toned physique without an extreme level of musculature.

In 2012, the Women's Physique category was introduced, focusing on a balance between muscle and aesthetics.

Social media played a crucial role in popularizing female bodybuilding, allowing bodybuilders to share their routines and competitions with a global audience.

In addition to Lisa Lyon and Rachel McLish, other influential bodybuilders include Cory Everson, who won six consecutive Ms. Olympia titles from 1984 to 1989, and Iris Kyle, who has won the Ms. Olympia title ten times, making her one of the most successful bodybuilders in history.

Despite challenges and controversies, female bodybuilding has grown significantly and gained acceptance in society.

Today, female bodybuilders are recognized for their dedication, strength, and achievements, and the sport continues to evolve with new categories and competitions.

The history of female bodybuilding is a journey of overcoming barriers and stereotypes, adapting and evolving over time to include a variety of categories that celebrate different forms of female strength and aesthetics.

26

The use of anabolic steroids in bodybuilding has been a controversial topic and, tragically, has led to the deaths of several bodybuilders.

- **Andreas Münzer:** An Austrian bodybuilder known for his extreme muscle definition and low body fat percentage, died in 1996 at the age of 31. His death was attributed to multiple organ failures, exacerbated by the use of steroids and diuretics. Münzer was famous for his strict diet and intensive use of substances to achieve his muscular appearance, which ultimately led to fatal complications.

- **Mohammed Benaziza:** Known as "The Killer of Giants" for defeating bodybuilders larger than himself, Mohammed Benaziza died in 1992 at the age of 33. After winning a competition in the Netherlands, Benaziza passed away due to heart failure attributed to the use of diuretics and other compounds. His death highlighted the dangers of excessive substance use to achieve extreme physical conditions.

- **Dallas McCarver:** A promising American bodybuilder, died in 2017 at the age of 26. His death was caused by a combination of heart problems and a tracheal obstruction. Significant levels of anabolic steroids were found in his system, suggesting that the use of these substances contributed to his health issues.

- **Rich Piana:** A bodybuilder and social media personality, died in 2017 at the age of 46 after collapsing at his home. Piana had been open about his use of steroids and other anabolic substances throughout his career. Although his official cause of death was heart disease, the prolonged use of steroids and other compounds undoubtedly contributed to his health problems.

- **Nasser El Sonbaty:** A highly successful professional bodybuilder, died in 2013 at the age of 47. His death is believed to have been caused by heart and kidney complications attributed to the use of steroids and other drugs throughout his career. El Sonbaty was known for his enormous size and muscular condition, achieved in part due to the use of these substances.

- **Mike Matarazzo:** A very popular professional bodybuilder in the 90s, died in 2014 at the age of 48 due to heart complications. Matarazzo had suffered multiple heart-related health issues and had spoken openly about the risks of using steroids and other compounds. His death underscores the long-term dangers associated with these substances.

- **Greg Kovacs:** Known for his colossal size, died in 2013 at the age of 44. Kovacs suffered a heart attack, and his prolonged use of anabolic steroids and other substances to maintain his extreme size was a contributing factor. His death highlighted the risks of pursuing extreme muscle sizes through the use of drugs.

- **Aziz Shavershian (Zyzz):** Although not a professional bodybuilder, Aziz Shavershian, known as "Zyzz," was a popular figure in the online fitness and bodybuilding community. He died in 2011 at the age of 22 due to a heart attack while on vacation in Thailand. It was found that the use of anabolic steroids had contributed to his death, underscoring the risks associated with these substances even for those who do not compete professionally.

- **Daniele Seccarecci:** An Italian bodybuilder, died in 2013 at the age of 33 due to a heart attack. Seccarecci had been recognized for his achievements in professional bodybuilding, but his use of steroids and other compounds was a factor in his premature death.

There are two main types of muscle hypertrophy: sarcoplasmic hypertrophy and myofibrillar hypertrophy.

Both types of hypertrophy contribute to an increase in muscle size, but they do so in different ways and respond to different types of training stimuli.

1. Sarcoplasmic hypertrophy: This is the increase in the volume of muscle cells due to an increase in the content of fluid and other non-contractile components within the muscle cell. This type of hypertrophy is characterized by a greater volume of sarcoplasm, the fluid that surrounds the myofibrils in muscle cells. As a result, the muscles look larger, but this does not always translate into a significant increase in muscle strength.

- **Mechanism:** Increase in cell fluid volume and storage of glycogen, water, and other nutrients in muscle cells.
- **Training:** To stimulate sarcoplasmic hypertrophy, it is recommended to train with repetition ranges between 8 and 15 reps per set with moderate intensity weight. This type of training induces a greater accumulation of metabolites (such as lactate), which can contribute to the increase of sarcoplasm.
- **Benefits:** Increases muscle endurance and the ability of muscles to store more glycogen, which can improve performance in endurance activities and high-volume training.

2. Myofibrillar hypertrophy: This is the increase in the size of muscle fibers due to the growth and proliferation of myofibrils, which are the contractile structures within muscle cells. This type of hypertrophy results in an increase in muscle strength and power.

- **Mechanism:** Increase in the number and size of myofibrils within muscle cells, enhancing their contractile capabilities.
- **Training:** To stimulate myofibrillar hypertrophy, it is recommended to train with lower repetition ranges (typically 4-6 reps per set) using heavier weights. This type of training focuses on lifting maximum weights to induce mechanical tension and muscle fiber recruitment.
- **Benefits:** Increases muscle strength, power, and overall force production, making it beneficial for activities that require maximal strength and explosive movements.

- **Mechanism:** Increase in the number and size of myofibrils within muscle cells, improving the muscle's contractile capacity.
- **Training:** To stimulate myofibrillar hypertrophy, it is recommended to train with high intensities and low repetitions, typically between 3 and 6 reps per set with heavy weights. This type of training places greater emphasis on mechanical overload and muscle tension.
- **Benefits:** Increases muscle strength and power, which is particularly beneficial for activities requiring explosiveness and heavy lifting.

Comparison and application in training:

Both types of hypertrophy are important for balanced and comprehensive muscle development.

Bodybuilders and athletes often incorporate training strategies that include both types of stimuli to maximize muscle growth and performance.

- **Periodized training:** Many training programs periodize phases of sarcoplasmic and myofibrillar hypertrophy. For example, they might include 4-6 week training blocks focused on higher repetition ranges (8-15) for sarcoplasmic hypertrophy, followed by training blocks with lower repetition ranges (3-6) for myofibrillar hypertrophy.
- **Hybrid training:** Another strategy is to combine both types of stimuli within the same session or training week. For example, performing heavy compound exercises with low repetitions at the beginning of the session (for myofibrillar hypertrophy) and following up with isolation exercises with moderate to high repetitions (for sarcoplasmic hypertrophy).

28

A bodybuilding training session should not last more than 90 minutes.

After this time, the body begins to experience a series of effects that can work against the goals of muscle growth and performance.

The main reason for keeping training sessions within this limit is due to hormonal factors, fatigue, and efficiency.

In terms of hormones, training beyond 90 minutes can result in an increase in the release of cortisol, a catabolic hormone that can break down muscle tissue and inhibit protein synthesis.

Cortisol rises in response to prolonged physical stress, and while moderate levels can be manageable, a significant increase can counteract the benefits of training by reducing the body's ability to build and repair muscle tissue.

Fatigue is another critical factor.

As the training session extends, energy levels decrease and the quality of performance can deteriorate.

This not only reduces the effectiveness of the training but also increases the risk of injury due to decreased concentration and form.

Mental and physical fatigue can lead to incorrect execution of exercises, which can cause short- and long-term damage.

From an efficiency standpoint, training for more than 90 minutes can be counterproductive in terms of time and effort invested.

The principle of progressive overload, which is essential for muscle growth, can be effectively achieved within a shorter period if the training is well-structured.

This includes an appropriate combination of intensity, volume, and rest between sets.

Maximizing intensity and focus during a shorter period can be more beneficial than unnecessarily prolonging the session.

Additionally, training for long periods can interfere with recovery.

Recovery is crucial for muscle growth, and the body needs time to repair and build the tissue damaged during training.

Excessively long workouts can reduce the quality of sleep and recovery time, which can negatively impact performance in future sessions.

Regarding nutrition, the body also requires a constant supply of nutrients to maintain performance and recovery.

During long training sessions, muscle glycogen levels can be depleted, reducing the energy available to continue training at high intensity.

Nutrient intake before and after training is crucial for replenishing these levels and supporting muscle recovery.

29

To optimize muscle gains and avoid plateaus, it is essential to introduce variations in training approximately every six weeks.

This strategy is based on the principle of periodization, which involves systematically changing training variables to keep the body constantly adapting and to avoid monotony.

The need for variation arises from several factors.

Firstly, the human body is incredibly efficient at adapting to repetitive stimuli.

If you perform the same exercises with the same volume and intensity over a prolonged period, your progress will eventually slow down or even stop due to muscle adaptation.

Changing training variables, such as exercises, volume, intensity, frequency, and training methods, forces the muscles to adapt to new challenges, promoting continuous growth.

An effective way to introduce variations is through periodization, which can be linear, nonlinear, or undulating.

Linear periodization involves progressively increasing training intensity while reducing volume.

For example, you might start with a focus on hypertrophy with repetition ranges of 8-12 and then switch to a strength focus with repetition ranges of 3-6.

Nonlinear or undulating periodization involves varying these variables more frequently, even weekly, to keep the body in a constant state of adaptation.

Another way to vary training is by changing exercises and introducing new movements or modifying existing ones to provide a different stimulus to the muscles.

For example, if you've been doing barbell bench presses, you can switch to dumbbell bench presses or incorporate isolation exercises like flyes.

Changing the angles of exercises can also be beneficial, such as alternating between incline and decline presses.

Volume and intensity are key variables that also need to be adjusted.

Over a six-week period, you could gradually increase volume (number of sets and repetitions) and then reduce it while increasing intensity (weight lifted).

This approach not only helps avoid overtraining but also ensures that muscles continue to be challenged in different ways.

Training frequency, or how many times you train each muscle group per week, can also be varied.

Some programs might start with a low frequency, training each muscle group once a week, and then increase to two or even three times a week to intensify the growth stimulus.

Incorporating different training methods, such as supersets, drop sets, forced reps, rest-pause training, and tempo training, can add a new challenge and promote additional adaptations.

These methods intensify the muscle stimulus and can help overcome progress plateaus.

30

Muscle soreness, commonly known as Delayed Onset Muscle Soreness (DOMS), is caused by microtrauma to muscle fibers.

This soreness typically occurs between 24 and 72 hours after performing intense or unusual exercise and is a natural response of the body to microscopic damage in muscle tissue.

The eccentric or negative part of an exercise, which involves lengthening the muscle while applying a load, is especially effective in causing this microtrauma.

During the eccentric phase, the muscle lengthens under tension, which places greater stress on the muscle fibers compared to the concentric phase (muscle shortening).

This additional stress causes a higher degree of microscopic damage, resulting in increased inflammation and subsequent muscle soreness.

The process of the body's repair and adaptation to these microtraumas is what ultimately leads to muscle growth and increased strength.

When damage occurs, the body responds by initiating an inflammatory process, which includes the arrival of immune cells to the damaged area to begin repair.

This repair not only fixes the damage but also strengthens the muscle tissue, making it stronger and more resistant to similar future damage.

The eccentric phase of an exercise can be emphasized in various ways to maximize its impact.

A common technique is to deliberately slow down the eccentric movement.

For example, in a bench press, lowering the bar slowly and in a controlled manner rather than letting it drop quickly can increase the time under tension and therefore the muscle damage.

Another technique is to use a higher weight than would normally be used for the concentric phase, as muscles are generally stronger in the eccentric phase.

While muscle soreness induced by eccentric exercise is a sign of muscle damage, it is not always an accurate indicator of the effectiveness of the workout.

It is possible to experience significant muscle growth without feeling extreme soreness.

Additionally, over time and with adaptation, the severity of DOMS can decrease, even if muscles continue to grow and strengthen.

To manage and minimize DOMS, a series of strategies is recommended.

Warming up before exercise can prepare the muscles and reduce the risk of severe damage.

After exercise, performing a cool-down routine, including light stretching and low-intensity activities, can help reduce muscle soreness.

Proper nutrition, especially protein and amino acid intake, is crucial for muscle repair.

Hydration also plays an important role in recovery.

Using active recovery methods, such as massage, compression therapy, and foam rolling, can relieve muscle soreness and speed up recovery.

Additionally, cold baths or contrast baths (alternating between cold and hot water) can reduce inflammation and pain.

It is important to note that while muscle soreness is an inevitable part of resistance training, it should not be the primary goal.

Excessively painful training can be indicative of overload or incorrect technique and can lead to long-term injuries if not properly managed.

31

The true definition of intensity in the context of strength training and bodybuilding refers to the percentage of your one-repetition maximum (1RM) that you are using in an exercise.

The 1RM is the maximum amount of weight you can lift in an exercise for a single repetition with proper technique.

Therefore, if you lift a weight that is 70% of your 1RM, you are working at 70% of your maximum intensity.

This concept of intensity is quantifiable and objective, unlike the subjective perception of how difficult a workout may feel.

While the rate of perceived exertion (RPE) can vary from person to person and can be influenced by factors such as fatigue, mental state, and environment, the percentage of 1RM provides a concrete and standardized measure of workload.

Working with different percentages of your 1RM has specific effects on the body and is used to achieve different training goals.

For example:

- 70-85% of 1RM: This range is generally used for hypertrophy training. Working in this intensity range promotes a balance between training volume and load, stimulating muscle growth.

- 85-100% of 1RM: This range is typically used for maximum strength training. Lifting loads close to your 1RM challenges the neuromuscular system and improves absolute strength.

- 50-70% of 1RM: This range is common in muscular endurance training and active recovery phases. Although the load is lower, the volume can be higher to maintain training intensity without overloading the nervous system.

Using the percentage of 1RM to define intensity also allows for more precise and structured training planning, known as periodization.

Periodization involves manipulating the intensity and volume of training in planned cycles to maximize gains and prevent plateaus.

For example, a linear periodization cycle might start with lighter loads (50-60% of 1RM) and gradually progress to heavier loads (85-95% of 1RM) over several weeks.

Measuring intensity as a percentage of 1RM is also essential for training safety.

Continuously training with very high loads (close to 100% of 1RM) without proper planning can increase the risk of injuries due to excessive stress on muscles, tendons, and joints.

By systematically varying intensity, the body is allowed to recover and adapt, reducing the risk of long-term injuries.

It is important to note that intensity based on the percentage of 1RM should be adjusted according to individual capacity and progress.

As a bodybuilder gains strength, their 1RM increases, and therefore, the weights used in training should also increase to maintain the same relative intensity.

This underscores the need for periodic evaluations of 1RM to appropriately adjust training loads.

In practice, many bodybuilders and trainers combine the use of percentage of 1RM with perceived exertion to design effective training programs.

While the percentage of 1RM provides an objective guide, perceived exertion allows for daily adjustments based on how the athlete feels on a given day.

This combination can help optimize performance and recovery.

32

Training the legs has a significant impact on overall strength and muscle size development due to various physiological and hormonal factors.

When training the legs, especially with compound and high-intensity exercises like squats and deadlifts, large muscle groups are stimulated, leading to a series of beneficial responses for the body as a whole.

One of the main benefits of training the legs is the stimulation of testosterone and growth hormone production.

These two are key anabolic hormones that play a crucial role in muscle protein synthesis and muscle growth.

Testosterone, in particular, is involved in increasing muscle mass and strength, while growth hormone contributes to tissue repair and cell regeneration.

Compound leg exercises, such as squats, lunges, and deadlifts, require coordinated effort from multiple large muscle groups, including the quadriceps, hamstrings, glutes, and lower back muscles.

This coordinated effort triggers a greater release of anabolic hormones compared to exercises that focus solely on the upper body.

The increased release of testosterone and growth hormone not only benefits the leg muscles but can also have a positive effect on muscle growth throughout the body.

In addition to hormonal responses, leg training enhances the body's overall load-bearing capacity and strength.

Strong legs provide a solid foundation and stability for performing other exercises more effectively.

For example, greater leg strength can improve performance in Olympic lifts and other compound movements that also involve the upper body.

This results in more balanced muscle development and an increase in overall strength.

Leg training can also contribute to an increase in lean body mass due to the large amount of muscle mass involved.

By developing large muscles in the legs, the body requires more energy and nutrients to maintain and repair these tissues, which can lead to higher calorie consumption and a more active metabolism.

This not only aids in muscle growth but can also facilitate fat loss, contributing to better body composition.

Another important aspect is the improvement in cardiovascular capacity and muscular endurance obtained through leg training.

Leg exercises are often physically demanding and can enhance cardiovascular capacity, allowing bodybuilders to train with greater intensity and volume overall.

This can increase work capacity and efficiency in training sessions, leading to greater muscle development.

In terms of injury prevention and muscular balance, training the legs is crucial for maintaining the body's stability and mobility.

A strong and balanced foundation in the legs reduces the risk of injuries in both the lower and upper body by improving body alignment and load distribution during movements.

33

Weightlifting should be viewed primarily as an activity intended to stimulate muscle growth rather than as a way to burn calories.

Although it is true that any physical activity consumes energy, the main purpose of weight training is to induce adaptations in muscle tissue that result in increased muscle mass, strength, and endurance.

During an intense weightlifting session, you can burn between 200 and 300 calories, depending on factors such as the intensity of the workout, the duration of the session, the type of exercises performed, the weight lifted, and the individual athlete's metabolism.

This caloric expenditure is relatively modest compared to aerobic activities like running or cycling, which can burn significantly more calories in the same period.

The true value of weightlifting lies in its ability to trigger the process of muscle hypertrophy.

Hypertrophy is achieved by creating microtraumas in the muscle fibers during exercise, which the body then repairs and strengthens during periods of rest and recovery.

This process not only increases the size and strength of the muscles but also raises the basal metabolic rate (BMR), the number of calories the body burns at rest.

The increase in muscle mass has a significant effect on metabolism.

Muscle tissue is metabolically active, meaning it requires more energy to maintain than fat tissue.

Therefore, as a person gains more muscle mass, their body burns more calories at rest.

This increase in basal metabolism can contribute to long-term fat loss, even though the primary goal of weightlifting is not the direct burning of calories during exercise.

Additionally, weight training induces the so-called "afterburn effect" or excess post-exercise oxygen consumption (EPOC).

After an intense weightlifting session, the body continues to burn calories at an elevated rate while repairing muscles and replenishing energy stores.

This effect can last several hours post-workout, further contributing to the total caloric expenditure.

To maximize the benefits of weightlifting in terms of muscle hypertrophy, it is crucial to focus on various aspects of training, such as progressive overload (gradually increasing the weight lifted), exercise variation (to avoid plateaus and work different parts of the muscle), proper volume and intensity (number of sets and repetitions), and incorporating advanced techniques (such as supersets, drop sets, and rest-pause training).

34

Alternating loads from one set to another, instead of following a traditional pyramid progression, can be an effective strategy for gaining more strength and volume in a bodybuilder's training.

This method, known as undulating load training or load variation, involves changing the weight lifted in each set within a single training session.

Advantages of alternating loads:

- **Diversification of muscle stimulus:** By varying loads between sets, a diverse stimulus is provided to the muscles, which can prevent plateaus and promote continuous muscle growth. Different weights and repetitions affect muscle fibers in various ways, which can maximize hypertrophy.
- **Optimization of fatigue and recovery:** Alternating between medium, light, and heavy weights in different sets can help manage fatigue. Sets with lighter weights can serve as a form of active recovery, allowing muscles to partially recover before facing heavier weights again.
- **Improvement of strength and endurance:** This method combines strength training (with heavy weights and low repetitions), hypertrophy training (with medium weights and moderate repetitions), and muscular endurance training (with light weights and high repetitions). This combination can improve maximum strength and muscular endurance simultaneously.
- **Greater muscle activation:** Alternating loads can engage different types of muscle fibers (fast and slow), resulting in greater activation and complete muscle development. Fast-twitch fibers, which are more responsible for strength and power, benefit from heavy weights, while slow-twitch fibers, more oriented towards endurance, respond better to light weights and high repetitions.

Implementation Strategies:

- **Undulating Series:** A common way to implement this method is by using undulating series within a training session. For example, you can perform the first set with a medium weight (70% of 1RM), the second set with a light weight (50-60% of 1RM), and the third set with a heavy weight (85-90% of 1RM).

- **Undulating Periodization:** This approach can also be applied in a weekly or monthly periodization scheme. For example, one training day can focus on heavy weights and low repetitions, another day on medium weights and moderate repetitions, and another day on light weights and high repetitions.

- **Load Cycling:** Another strategy is to cycle the loads within the same training week, where each session has a different focus but all focuses alternate in each session. This could look like one session focused on strength (heavy weights), one on hypertrophy (medium weights), and one on endurance (light weights).

Training Example.

Suppose you are training the chest:

- **First Set:** Medium weight (70% of 1RM) - 8-10 repetitions.
- **Second Set:** Light weight (50-60% of 1RM) - 12-15 repetitions.
- **Third Set:** Heavy weight (85-90% of 1RM) - 4-6 repetitions.

This approach can be applied to various exercises within a single session or to different exercises for a specific muscle group.

35

High-Intensity Interval Training (HIIT) is an effective strategy for preserving muscle mass and staying lean while utilizing time efficiently.

HIIT involves alternating periods of high-intensity exercise with periods of rest or low-intensity exercise.

This approach is not only beneficial for burning fat but can also help maintain and improve muscle mass due to several physiological factors.

One of the main benefits of HIIT is its ability to burn a large number of calories in a short period.

HIIT sessions typically last between 20 and 30 minutes, making them ideal for people with busy schedules who want to maximize their workout efficiency.

During high-intensity intervals, the body works at near-maximal capacity, which increases metabolism and post-exercise oxygen consumption (EPOC).

This "afterburn" effect means that the body continues to burn calories at an elevated rate for several hours after the workout.

HIIT also helps preserve muscle mass while losing fat.

Unlike traditional steady-state cardiovascular exercises, which can lead to muscle loss if done excessively, HIIT workouts include brief bursts of anaerobic exercise that stimulate fast-twitch muscle fibers.

This not only helps maintain muscle mass but can also improve muscle strength and power.

Additionally, HIIT can induce the release of anabolic hormones such as testosterone and growth hormone, which are crucial for maintaining and developing muscle mass.

These hormones promote protein synthesis and muscle repair, helping to counteract any potential muscle breakdown that might occur during calorie burning.

The variety of exercises that can be incorporated into a HIIT session also contributes to its effectiveness.

Compound exercises and movements involving multiple muscle groups, such as sprints, burpees, jumps, weightlifting, and plyometric exercises, can be included.

This not only increases the intensity of the workout but also ensures that various muscles are worked, promoting balanced and comprehensive development.

For bodybuilders, HIIT can perfectly complement resistance training.

By performing HIIT sessions on alternate days or as a supplement after weight training, fat burning can be maximized without compromising muscle growth.

Furthermore, the improvement in cardiovascular capacity and endurance obtained through HIIT can benefit weight training sessions, allowing for greater work capacity and better recovery between sets.

Another important aspect of HIIT is its adaptability.

HIIT sessions can be adjusted to different fitness levels and specific goals.

For example, a beginner might start with intervals of 20 seconds of high intensity followed by 40 seconds of rest, while a more advanced athlete might opt for intervals of 30 seconds of high intensity with 30 seconds of rest.

The flexibility of HIIT allows for gradual progression and continuous adjustment to keep the body challenged and prevent plateaus.

Additionally, HIIT can be performed in a variety of settings, whether in a gym, outdoors, or even at home with the right equipment.

This makes it accessible and convenient for virtually anyone, regardless of their resources or time constraints.

In terms of efficiency, HIIT not only saves time but can also be more effective in terms of results compared to traditional long-duration cardiovascular workouts.

The intensity and effort required for HIIT workouts can produce significant improvements in body composition, cardiovascular health, and metabolic capacity in a relatively short period.

36

Increasing muscle activation when lifting weights by crushing the bar or dumbbells is a technique that enhances muscle tension by applying force not only to lift the weight but also to actively "crush" or compress the bar or dumbbells.

This approach can intensify muscular effort and improve the activation of various muscle fibers, potentially leading to more effective muscle growth and increased strength.

When you crush the bar or dumbbells, you engage additional muscles and increase stability during the exercise.

This principle is based on irradiation, a neuromuscular phenomenon where the activation of one muscle group can increase the activation of adjacent muscles.

For example, crushing the bar during a bench press activates not only the chest muscles but also the shoulder muscles, triceps, and even core muscles.

The technique of crushing the bar or dumbbells can be particularly effective in several key exercises:

- **Bench Press:** By squeezing the bar, you increase the activation of the pectorals, triceps, and deltoids, enhancing shoulder stability and allowing for a more controlled and powerful lift. This technique can also help protect the shoulders by maintaining proper alignment.
- **Bicep Curl:** By crushing the dumbbells, you intensify the contraction in the biceps and forearm muscles, leading to greater muscle activation and consequently more growth.
- **Military Press:** Squeezing the bar while performing a military press can increase stability and the activation of the deltoids, triceps, and core stabilizer muscles, improving the efficiency of the lift.

- **Barbell Row:** Squeezing the bar during a row intensifies the contraction of the back muscles, biceps, and forearms, which can enhance muscle strength and size.
- **Barbell Squat:** Crushing the bar against your back during a squat improves core stability and can increase the activation of core muscles, helping to maintain proper posture and lift more weight safely.

Benefits of Crushing the Bar or Dumbbells:

- **Increased Muscle Activation:** The technique of crushing the bar or dumbbells creates greater tension in the target muscles and stabilizing muscles, leading to higher activation and recruitment of muscle fibers.
- **Improved Stability and Control:** This technique helps improve joint stability and neuromuscular control during lifts, reducing the risk of injury and allowing for more efficient lifting.
- **Strength Development:** By increasing muscle tension and activation, strength levels can improve. Continuous practice of this technique can lead to significant increases in both maximum and relative strength.
- **Enhanced Muscle Growth:** Increased muscle activation and tension can stimulate greater hypertrophic responses due to higher mechanical and metabolic stress on the muscles.

37

**Whatever training you choose,
it is crucial to give it enough time to work.**

In the context of bodybuilding, this means allowing the body to go through the adaptation process, which typically takes at least six weeks before noticeable results are visible.

This adaptation period is necessary for the muscles, tendons, ligaments, and central nervous system to get accustomed to the new demands imposed by the training program.

The adaptation process includes several stages.

Initially, the muscles experience microtrauma during training, triggering a repair and growth response.

During the first few weeks, changes may not be visibly evident, but at the cellular and neuromuscular levels, the body is adjusting to better handle the stress of training.

This process also involves improvements in the efficiency of muscle fiber recruitment, intramuscular coordination, and strength.

Consistency in training is more effective for achieving long-term gains than extremely intense workouts performed over a short period.

Highly intense workouts can quickly lead to overtraining, fatigue, and injury risk.

Overtraining occurs when the body does not have enough time to adequately recover between training sessions, which can lead to a decrease in performance and potential long-term damage.

On the other hand, consistency in training allows the body to recover and adapt gradually.

Maintaining a well-structured and consistent training program promotes gradual and sustainable progression.

This approach ensures that the muscles receive adequate stimulus for growth while minimizing the risk of excessive fatigue and injuries.

Additionally, consistency allows bodybuilders to monitor their progress and adjust training as necessary to keep advancing.

Gains in strength and muscle size require a long-term approach.

This includes not only regular training but also attention to other crucial factors such as proper nutrition, rest, and recovery.

A balanced diet rich in proteins, carbohydrates, and healthy fats is essential to provide the necessary nutrients for muscle repair and growth.

Furthermore, sleep and rest are fundamental to allow the body to recover and adapt to training.

Patience and discipline are key virtues in bodybuilding.

It is easy to become demotivated if immediate results are not seen, but it is important to remember that muscle growth is a gradual process.

Significant changes in body composition and strength can take months or even years of consistent and dedicated training.

Additionally, periodically varying the training program can help maintain progress.

After an initial period of six weeks, it may be beneficial to introduce changes in volume, intensity, exercises, and training frequency to keep challenging the body and avoid plateaus.

This technique, known as periodization, allows bodybuilders to continue progressing by providing new stimuli and preventing complete adaptation to a specific training regimen.

38

The SAID principle (Specific Adaptation to Imposed Demands) is a fundamental principle in bodybuilding and other sports disciplines.

This principle states that the body specifically adapts to the demands placed on it.

In other words, the muscles and body systems adapt specifically to the types of training and stress they are subjected to.

Therefore, to optimize results, it is crucial to focus training on one or two main objectives rather than trying to improve all athletic qualities simultaneously.

1. Training Specificity:
The SAID principle underscores the importance of specificity in training. If your main goal is muscle hypertrophy (muscle growth), your training program should focus on methods and techniques that maximize hypertrophy. This includes working in repetition ranges typically between 6 and 12, using moderate to heavy loads, and ensuring an adequate training volume.
On the other hand, if your goal is to increase maximum strength, your training should include lifts with weights close to your maximum, generally in the range of 1 to 5 repetitions, with a greater emphasis on load and intensity than on total volume.

2. Limitation of Objectives:
Training for multiple goals simultaneously can dilute the effects of each and lead to suboptimal results.
For example, trying to improve cardiovascular endurance while maximizing muscle hypertrophy at the same time can be counterproductive. Intense and frequent cardiovascular training can interfere with strength and muscle growth adaptations due to competition for recovery resources and potential interference with muscle protein synthesis signals.

3. Periodization and Training Cycles:

To address different goals without compromising results, bodybuilders and athletes often use periodization. Periodization involves dividing training into specific cycles, each focused on a particular goal. For example, you might have an 8-12 week hypertrophy cycle followed by a 6-8 week strength cycle. This approach allows the body to adapt specifically to one set of demands before shifting the focus to another goal, maximizing adaptations for each quality.

4. Example of Applying the SAID Principle:

- **Hypertrophy:** If your goal is muscle hypertrophy, focus on compound and isolation exercises, working in moderate repetition ranges (6-12), with high training volume and moderate rest periods (60-90 seconds). Nutrition should support protein synthesis with adequate calorie and macronutrient intake.

- **Strength:** If your goal is strength, incorporate heavy lifts with low repetitions (1-5), longer rest periods (2-5 minutes), and a focus on technique and load progression. Ensure sufficient recovery time between strength training sessions.

- **Muscular Endurance:** If your goal is muscular endurance, use lighter weights with higher repetitions (15-20 or more), short rest periods (30-60 seconds), and increased training frequency.

5. Benefits of Specificity:

Training specificity not only optimizes physical adaptations but also facilitates planning and tracking progress. With clear and specific goals, it is easier to design effective training programs and adjust variables (such as intensity, volume, and frequency) to achieve those goals. Additionally, specificity can help prevent overtraining and injuries, as the body adapts more efficiently to a limited set of demands rather than facing multiple competing stressors.

6. Avoid Extensive Cross-Training:

While cross-training can have benefits, in the context of bodybuilding, it's important to avoid an overly broad approach that attempts to improve all athletic qualities at once.

A more effective approach is to incorporate complementary exercises that support the main goal without interfering with it. For example, a bodybuilder aiming for hypertrophy can include low-intensity cardio sessions to improve cardiovascular health without compromising muscle adaptations.

39

Properly cooling down after a training session is crucial for a bodybuilder, as it helps prevent muscles from shortening and becoming stiff.

Lack of adequate cooling down can lead to a buildup of muscle tension, stiffness, and increased susceptibility to injuries.

Performing some form of light exercise and flexibility work after training provides numerous benefits that support recovery and long-term performance.

Benefits of Cooling Down.

- Reduction of heart rate and blood pressure: Cooling down helps the heart gradually return to its normal rhythm after intense exercise. This is important to avoid a sudden drop in blood pressure, which can cause dizziness or fainting.

- Prevention of lactic acid buildup: Light exercise after training helps eliminate metabolic byproducts, such as lactic acid, that accumulate in the muscles during intense exercise. This reduces post-workout muscle stiffness and soreness (DOMS).

- Improvement of flexibility: Incorporating stretching exercises during the cool-down can help maintain and improve muscle flexibility. This is essential to prevent muscles from shortening and becoming stiff. Static stretches are particularly effective for this purpose, as they allow the muscle to relax and lengthen.

- **Facilitation of muscle recovery:** Cooling down improves blood circulation, which facilitates the delivery of oxygen and nutrients to muscles and tissues, accelerating the process of muscle recovery and repair.

- **Reduction of injury risk:** Muscle stiffness and tension can increase the risk of injuries. Proper cooling down and flexibility work help keep muscles loose and prepared for the next training session, reducing the risk of tears, sprains, and other injuries.

Components of Proper Cooling Down

- **Light aerobic exercise:** Perform 5 to 10 minutes of low-intensity aerobic exercise, such as walking, gentle jogging, or cycling, to gradually reduce heart rate and body temperature.

- **Static stretching:** After light aerobic exercise, spend 10 to 15 minutes on static stretches. These stretches should be held for at least 20-30 seconds each, focusing on the muscle groups worked during the training session. Common stretches include hamstring, quadriceps, glutes, pectorals, lats, and triceps stretches.

- **Mobility exercises:** In addition to static stretches, including mobility exercises can help maintain joint range of motion. This can include controlled, gentle movements such as shoulder circles, leg swings, and hip rotations.

- **Breathing techniques:** Incorporating deep breathing techniques during cooling down can help relax the nervous system and reduce stress. Deep, controlled breathing improves muscle oxygenation and can facilitate overall body relaxation.

- **Post-workout hydration and nutrition:** Staying hydrated and consuming a meal or shake rich in protein and carbohydrates after training is also essential for recovery. Proper hydration helps maintain muscle elasticity and prevent cramps, while nutrients facilitate muscle repair and growth.

Implementation in the training routine

To implement proper cooling down in the training routine, it is important to plan it as an integral part of each session. It should not be considered an optional activity, but an essential part of the training program.

Example of how cooling down could be structured:

- **Light aerobic exercise:** 5-10 minutes of walking on the treadmill or gentle jogging.
- **Static stretching:** 10-15 minutes of stretching, covering all the major muscle groups worked.
- **Mobility exercises:** 5 minutes of joint mobility movements.
- **Breathing techniques:** 2-3 minutes of deep, controlled breathing.

40

Time Under Tension (TUT) is a crucial factor in muscle development and refers to the total time a muscle is under load during a series of exercises.

TUT is important because it directly influences the degree of mechanical and metabolic stress that muscle fibers experience, which is essential for promoting muscle hypertrophy.

When muscles spend more time under tension, microtraumas occur in the muscle fibers, triggering a repair and growth response.

This process, known as muscle protein synthesis, is fundamental for increasing muscle size.

A greater TUT can lead to a higher accumulation of metabolites such as lactate, hydrogen ions, and inorganic phosphate, which also contribute to the signaling of anabolic pathways and muscle growth.

To optimize TUT, it is useful to control the speed of repetitions, dividing them into concentric (contraction), eccentric (lengthening), and isometric (pause) phases.

The eccentric phase is especially important, as the controlled lengthening of the muscle under load causes significant muscle damage that stimulates growth.

For example, in a bicep curl, you can lift the weight (concentric phase) in 1-2 seconds, lower the weight (eccentric phase) in 3-4 seconds, and hold a contraction (isometric phase) for 1 second at the highest point.

Working with different TUTs can help target different types of muscle fibers.

Slow-twitch fibers (Type I) respond well to longer TUT with light to moderate weights and high repetitions, while fast-twitch fibers (Type II) are activated with shorter TUT, heavier weights, and low to moderate repetitions.

Focusing on TUT can also influence the total training volume, as increasing time under tension may require adjusting the number of sets and repetitions to avoid overtraining.

Incorporating techniques such as drop sets, forced repetitions, and rest-pause training can help manipulate TUT to maximize muscle stress and promote hypertrophy.

The use of TUT should be consistent with the training goals and the periodization of the program.

During hypertrophy phases, a TUT of 30-70 seconds per set is generally effective.

In strength phases, the TUT can be shorter due to the higher load and lower number of repetitions.

It is important to vary the TUT over time to maintain a constant stimulus and avoid plateaus.

Besides the direct impact on muscle growth, TUT also has indirect benefits, such as improving muscular endurance and neuromuscular coordination.

Muscles accustomed to working under prolonged tension develop a greater capacity to resist fatigue, which can enhance performance in other aspects of training.

41

The most anabolic hormone in the body is insulin, not testosterone.

Insulin plays a crucial role in muscle growth and repair as it facilitates the uptake of glucose and amino acids into muscle cells, promoting protein synthesis and glycogen storage.

Although testosterone is important for muscle hypertrophy due to its ability to increase protein synthesis and muscle mass, insulin is fundamental for the regulation of energy and anabolic metabolism.

To maximize the anabolic effects of insulin, it is essential to maintain insulin sensitivity.

Insulin sensitivity refers to how efficiently the body's cells respond to insulin.

High insulin sensitivity means that cells can use glucose more effectively, which is beneficial for both overall health and muscle growth.

Controlling carbohydrate intake is a key strategy for maintaining insulin sensitivity.

Some recommendations to achieve this:

- Consumption of complex carbohydrates:
Opt for complex carbohydrates such as oats, brown rice, sweet potatoes, legumes, and vegetables. These foods have a lower glycemic index and are digested slowly, helping to maintain stable blood sugar levels and prevent insulin spikes.

- **Carbohydrate distribution:** Spread carbohydrate intake throughout the day instead of consuming large amounts in one meal. This can help prevent large insulin spikes and maintain insulin sensitivity.

- **Pre- and post-workout meals:** Consume carbohydrates before and after workouts to maximize the anabolic response of insulin. Pre-workout carbohydrates provide energy, while post-workout carbohydrates help replenish muscle glycogen and promote recovery.

- **Macronutrient combination:** Combine carbohydrates with proteins and healthy fats in each meal. Proteins and fats slow down the digestion and absorption of carbohydrates, helping to maintain stable blood sugar levels.

- **Regular exercise:** Regular exercise, especially resistance training, improves insulin sensitivity. Strength training and aerobic exercise increase glucose uptake by muscles and enhance insulin function.

- **Stress control:** Chronic stress can negatively affect insulin sensitivity. Practices such as meditation, yoga, and deep breathing can help reduce stress and improve insulin sensitivity.

- **Supplementation:** Some supplements, such as alpha-lipoic acid, cinnamon, and chromium, can help improve insulin sensitivity. However, it is important to consult a healthcare professional before starting any supplementation regimen.

- **Avoid excess sugar and processed foods:** Limit the consumption of simple sugars and processed foods, which can cause rapid insulin spikes and contribute to insulin resistance.

42

Hydrolyzed whey protein is one of the fastest-absorbing forms of protein.

This type of protein is produced through a process that breaks down the proteins into smaller peptides, making it easier for the body to digest and absorb.

Due to its rapid absorption, hydrolyzed whey protein is ideal for consumption after workouts when muscles are most receptive to nutrients.

After an intense workout, the body enters a catabolic state where muscle fibers are worn down and glycogen levels are depleted.

Consuming a fast-absorbing protein like hydrolyzed whey quickly provides the necessary amino acids to initiate the repair and muscle protein synthesis process.

This helps facilitate recovery and muscle development.

Hydrolyzed whey protein not only absorbs quickly but is also rich in essential amino acids, including branched-chain amino acids (BCAAs) such as leucine, isoleucine, and valine.

These amino acids play a crucial role in stimulating muscle protein synthesis.

Leucine, in particular, is known for its ability to activate the mTOR pathway, a critical pathway in the muscle-building process.

To maximize the benefits of fast-absorbing protein post-workout, it is recommended to consume it within 30 minutes after exercise.

This period is known as the "anabolic window," during which the body is particularly efficient at absorbing and utilizing nutrients for recovery and muscle growth.

Although hydrolyzed whey protein is highly effective, it is not the only option.

Other fast-absorbing protein forms include whey protein isolate and certain types of hydrolyzed plant protein, which can also be effective for post-workout recovery.

In addition to protein, it is beneficial to consume carbohydrates along with protein after training.

Carbohydrates help replenish muscle glycogen stores, enhancing recovery and preparing the body for the next training session.

A combination of fast-absorbing protein and carbohydrates can maximize muscle protein synthesis and recovery.

It is important to note that the quality and total amount of protein consumed throughout the day also play a crucial role in muscle development.

While fast-absorbing protein post-workout is important, ensuring adequate protein intake at all meals helps maintain a positive nitrogen balance, essential for muscle growth.

43

If you weight train regularly, it is recommended to consume around one gram of protein for every half kilogram of body weight each day.

This equates to approximately 2.2 grams of protein per kilogram of body weight.

This amount of protein is essential to support muscle protein synthesis, tissue repair, and muscle growth, especially in individuals who engage in regular resistance training.

Adequate protein intake is crucial to maximizing the results of weight training.

Proteins are composed of amino acids, which are the building blocks of muscles.

During weight training, microtraumas occur in the muscle fibers.

Consuming enough protein ensures that the body has the resources needed to repair and build new, larger, and stronger muscle fibers.

For an individual who weighs 70 kilograms (154 pounds), this means they should consume approximately 154 grams of protein per day.

This amount can vary slightly based on individual factors such as training intensity, specific goals (muscle gain, maintenance, fat loss), and overall physical activity level.

Protein sources can include both animal and plant proteins.

Animal proteins, such as meat, fish, eggs, and dairy products, are considered complete proteins because they contain all essential amino acids in adequate proportions.

Plant proteins, such as legumes, nuts, seeds, and grains, can also provide adequate protein, but sometimes need to be combined to ensure a complete amino acid profile.

Distributing protein intake throughout the day in several meals can be more beneficial than consuming large amounts at once.

Including a source of protein in each meal and snack helps maintain a constant supply of amino acids for muscle protein synthesis.

This also helps maintain satiety and stable energy levels.

After training, it is particularly important to consume an adequate amount of protein.

During the "anabolic window," which is the period immediately following exercise, muscles are more receptive to nutrients.

Consuming a mix of protein and carbohydrates post-workout can maximize muscle repair and growth.

Some individuals, such as advanced bodybuilders or elite athletes, may need to adjust this amount according to their specific needs and training intensity.

In some cases, slightly higher amounts of protein may be recommended.

44

If you have ever taken a pre-workout supplement and felt a tingling sensation in your face, it is likely due to the presence of a specific ingredient, which could be niacin (vitamin B3), beta-alanine, or a combination of both.

Niacin, or vitamin B3, is a common ingredient in pre-workout supplements due to its role in improving blood flow and energy production.

Niacin can cause an effect known as "flush," characterized by a sensation of warmth, redness, and tingling in the skin, especially in the face and neck.

This effect is due to the dilation of blood vessels and the increased blood flow near the skin's surface.

Although niacin flush is harmless and temporary, it can be uncomfortable for some people.

However, it is more common for the tingling in the face from taking a pre-workout supplement to be caused by beta-alanine.

Beta-alanine is an amino acid used in pre-workout supplements to increase carnosine levels in muscles, helping to improve performance and delay muscle fatigue.

Beta-alanine can cause a tingling sensation known as paresthesia, which is a temporary and safe reaction.

This tingling sensation usually occurs when taking higher doses of beta-alanine and can be felt in the face, neck, hands, and feet.

The paresthesia caused by beta-alanine is the result of the activation of nerve receptors under the skin.

Although this sensation can be uncomfortable for some, it is not harmful and tends to subside as the body becomes accustomed to the supplement or if the dosage is reduced.

Both ingredients, niacin and beta-alanine, are used in pre-workout supplements for their performance benefits.

Niacin enhances energy production and blood flow, while beta-alanine helps improve muscular endurance and performance in high-intensity exercises.

However, the tingling or flush reaction can be more pronounced if the supplement contains high concentrations of these ingredients.

For those who find the tingling sensation uncomfortable, several strategies can be employed:

- **Adjust the dosage:** Reducing the amount of pre-workout supplement or splitting the dose throughout the day can minimize the tingling sensation.

- **Take with food:** Consuming the supplement with a meal can mitigate the effects of niacin and beta-alanine.

- **Use controlled-release supplements:**
Some supplements are formulated to release niacin or beta-alanine gradually, which can reduce the intensity of the tingling.

45

Hydration is crucial for optimal performance during exercise and muscle development.

Water plays multiple essential roles in the body, including regulating body temperature, lubricating joints, and transporting nutrients and oxygen to cells.

Staying well-hydrated is vital for overall health, but it is especially important for those engaging in intense physical activities like weight training.

During exercise, the body loses water through sweat, which can lead to dehydration if not replenished adequately.

Dehydration, even at moderate levels, can negatively impact physical and mental performance.

It can cause fatigue, reduce strength and endurance capacity, and increase the risk of injuries.

Additionally, dehydration can hinder muscle recovery by affecting the body's ability to transport nutrients and remove metabolic waste products.

The goal of drinking a gallon of water a day, approximately 3.8 liters, is a common recommendation to ensure adequate hydration; however, exact water needs may vary based on individual factors such as body size, activity level, climate, and diet.

Athletes and bodybuilders may need more water due to the higher fluid loss during intense exercise.

Water consumption should be spread throughout the day to maintain a constant level of hydration.

Drinking large amounts of water in a short period is not as effective as maintaining a consistent intake.

In addition to drinking water, consuming foods rich in water, such as fruits and vegetables, can significantly contribute to hydration.

During exercise, it is important to drink water before, during, and after physical activity.

Before exercise, a good practice is to consume 500-600 ml of water a few hours before starting.

During exercise, it is recommended to drink small amounts of water regularly, approximately every 15-20 minutes, to replenish fluids lost through sweat.

After exercise, it is crucial to continue hydrating to aid in recovery.

Proper hydration also has a direct impact on muscle protein synthesis and muscle growth, as the metabolic processes that facilitate the repair and growth of muscle tissue require a well-hydrated environment to function optimally.

Dehydration can slow these processes and limit muscle gains.

Additionally, hydration influences digestion and nutrient absorption, as water helps break down food and facilitates nutrient absorption in the intestine.

Good hydration ensures that essential nutrients, such as proteins, vitamins, and minerals, are efficiently absorbed, which is crucial for recovery and muscle development.

Drinking enough water also helps maintain the balance of electrolytes in the body.

Electrolytes, such as sodium, potassium, calcium, and magnesium, are necessary for muscle contractions and other physiological functions.

Dehydration can disrupt the balance of electrolytes, leading to muscle cramps and decreased performance.

46

Low levels of vitamin D have been associated with lower testosterone levels, which can negatively impact health and physical performance.

Vitamin D is a fat-soluble vitamin obtained from two main sources: sunlight exposure and dietary foods or supplements.

This vitamin plays a crucial role in regulating various bodily processes, including maintaining healthy hormone levels.

The relationship between vitamin D and testosterone has been widely researched.

Studies have shown that men with adequate vitamin D levels tend to have higher testosterone levels, while men with vitamin D deficiency tend to have lower levels of this hormone.

Testosterone is essential for muscle development, strength, libido, and bone health.

Low testosterone levels can lead to decreased muscle mass, fatigue, increased body fat, and other health problems.

Vitamin D can influence testosterone in several ways.

First, vitamin D can act directly on the testosterone-producing cells in the testes, stimulating the production of this hormone.

Additionally, vitamin D has anti-inflammatory and antioxidant properties that can improve overall health and endocrine function, which in turn can support optimal hormone levels.

To maintain adequate vitamin D levels, it is essential to ensure sufficient intake through sun exposure and/or supplements.

The skin produces vitamin D when exposed to sunlight, specifically UVB rays.

Spending time outdoors in direct sunlight, especially during midday hours, can help increase vitamin D levels.

Generally, it is recommended to spend 10 to 30 minutes in the sun several times a week, but for those living in areas with little sunlight or during the winter months, vitamin D supplements can be an effective option.

The supplementation dosage can vary, but generally, 1000 to 4000 IU of vitamin D3 per day is recommended, depending on an individual's current levels and medical advice.

In addition to sunlight and supplements, certain foods can also provide vitamin D. These include fatty fish such as salmon, mackerel, and sardines, as well as beef liver, cheese, egg yolks, and fortified foods like milk and cereals.

It is important to monitor vitamin D levels through blood tests, especially if a deficiency is suspected.

An adequate vitamin D level in the blood is generally considered to be between 30 and 60 ng/mL, but levels below 20 ng/mL are considered deficient and may require medical intervention to correct.

Vitamin D deficiency not only affects testosterone levels but can also have other health implications.

It can contribute to lower bone density, increasing the risk of osteoporosis and fractures, and has also been associated with a higher risk of cardiovascular diseases, immune problems, and certain types of cancer.

47

Casein protein is a slow-digesting protein predominantly found in dairy products, such as milk and cheese.

This slow-digesting property makes it optimal for consumption before bedtime, as it provides a steady supply of amino acids to the body during the overnight fasting period.

- Casein and Its Slow Digestion: Casein forms a gel in the stomach once consumed, which slows down its rate of digestion and absorption. This contrasts with whey protein, which digests quickly. Due to this prolonged digestion, casein can release amino acids into the bloodstream steadily over several hours, typically 6 to 8 hours. This extended release is beneficial for preventing muscle breakdown during sleep and promoting muscle protein synthesis.

- Benefits of Casein Before Bed: Taking casein before bed can be especially useful for athletes and bodybuilders looking to maximize recovery and muscle growth. During sleep, the body enters a state of repair and recovery. Providing a steady source of amino acids helps ensure that the body has the necessary nutrients for this process. This can lead to better muscle mass retention and increased muscle protein synthesis, which is crucial for hypertrophy and muscle recovery.

- **Comparison with Other Proteins:** While whey protein is excellent for rapid post-workout absorption due to its quick digestion and high concentration of branched-chain amino acids (BCAAs), casein is superior for nighttime use due to its slow release. Combining them at different times of the day can offer a comprehensive nutritional strategy to maximize muscle growth and recovery.

- **Sources of Casein:** Casein is naturally found in dairy products. Foods rich in casein include milk, yogurt, cottage cheese, and other cheeses. Casein supplements, typically in the form of micellar casein, are also available and can be a convenient option for those looking for a concentrated protein source before bedtime.

- **Consumption Strategy:** To take advantage of the benefits of casein before bed, it is recommended to consume a serving of casein (approximately 20-40 grams) 30-60 minutes before sleeping. This can be in the form of a casein protein shake or a casein-rich food like cottage cheese. This approach ensures that amino acid levels in the bloodstream remain elevated throughout the night, supporting muscle recovery.

- **Impact on Metabolism and Body Composition:** In addition to its benefits for muscle protein synthesis and preventing muscle breakdown, casein may also positively impact metabolism and body composition. Some studies suggest that consuming casein before bed can increase basal metabolic rate and improve fat oxidation, contributing to better body composition over time.

48

Creatine monohydrate is one of the most researched supplements and has consistently been shown to increase muscle size and strength.

Creatine is a natural substance found in small amounts in foods like red meat and fish and is also produced in the body from amino acids.

Creatine monohydrate, the most commonly used form in supplements, is considered highly effective and safe for enhancing physical performance and promoting muscle growth.

Creatine monohydrate works primarily by increasing phosphocreatine stores in the muscles.

Phosphocreatine is a rapid source of energy that muscle cells can use during high-intensity, short-duration exercises, such as weightlifting and sprints.

By increasing phosphocreatine stores, creatine allows athletes to perform more work at a higher intensity, leading to greater muscle overload and consequently, greater gains in muscle strength and size.

Numerous studies have shown that supplementation with creatine monohydrate can significantly improve muscle strength, power, and performance in high-intensity exercises.

These effects translate into a greater ability to lift heavier weights and perform more repetitions, which is crucial for muscle hypertrophy development.

Additionally, creatine has also shown benefits in muscle recovery, reducing the time needed to recover between sets and training sessions.

The use of creatine monohydrate is also associated with an increase in intracellular water content, which can contribute to greater muscle volume.

This "cell volumization" effect not only increases the apparent size of muscles but also can enhance the anabolic environment within muscle cells, promoting greater protein synthesis and thus muscle growth.

Creatine is especially effective when used in combination with a well-structured resistance training program.

To maximize its benefits, an initial loading protocol of 20 grams per day (divided into 4 doses of 5 grams) for 5-7 days is often recommended, followed by a maintenance phase of 3-5 grams per day.

However, some studies suggest that the loading phase may not be necessary and that a constant daily dose of 3-5 grams can also be effective in the long term.

Creatine monohydrate has been extensively researched and shown to be safe for long-term consumption in healthy individuals.

Unlike other supplements that may have significant side effects, creatine has been primarily associated with minor and transient side effects, such as gastrointestinal discomfort, which are usually mitigated by adjusting the dose or form of administration.

In addition to its benefits for physical performance and muscle growth, creatine has also shown positive effects on neurological and cognitive health.

Recent research suggests that creatine may play a role in protecting against neurodegenerative diseases and improving cognitive function, extending its usefulness beyond the realm of sports and fitness.

49

**Medium-chain triglycerides, or MCTs,
are a type of fat found in coconut oil,
palm oil, and butter from grass-fed animals.**

MCTs are an instant and easily digestible energy source due to their unique chemical structure.

Unlike long-chain triglycerides (LCTs), MCTs have shorter fatty acid chains, allowing them to be absorbed and metabolized more quickly by the body.

MCTs mainly consist of four types of fatty acids: caproic acid (C6), caprylic acid (C8), capric acid (C10), and lauric acid (C12).

Among these, caprylic acid (C8) and capric acid (C10) are the most valued for their ability to provide quick energy.

These fatty acids are transported directly to the liver after digestion, where they are rapidly converted into ketones, an energy source that can be used by the brain and muscles, especially in the absence of glucose.

Due to their rapid conversion into energy, MCTs are popular among athletes and people following ketogenic or low-carb diets.

MCTs can help increase energy, improve physical and mental performance, and support weight loss by enhancing thermogenesis (the production of heat in the body) and fat oxidation.

MCTs are also beneficial for digestion and nutrient absorption.

They are less likely to be stored as fat in the body and are efficiently used as an energy source.

Additionally, MCTs can have antimicrobial and antifungal properties, especially lauric acid, which can help fight infections and improve gut health.

Incorporating MCTs into the diet is relatively easy.

Coconut oil is a rich source of MCTs and can be used in cooking or as an additive in beverages and smoothies.

Concentrated MCT oil, available as a supplement, provides a purer and more concentrated form of these triglycerides and can be added to coffee, smoothies, or consumed directly.

Butter from grass-fed animals also contains MCTs, though in smaller amounts than coconut oil or concentrated MCT oil.

When using MCTs, it is important to start with small doses to allow the digestive system to adapt, as consuming large amounts of MCTs at once can cause gastrointestinal discomfort, such as diarrhea or stomach cramps.

Gradually increasing the dose can help minimize these effects.

50

Highly branched cyclic dextrin (HBCD) is a type of complex carbohydrate derived from starch that is characterized by its rapid digestion and absorption.

HBCD is known for its ability to efficiently replenish muscle glycogen stores, making it a popular supplement among athletes and bodybuilders looking to optimize recovery and performance.

HBCD is manufactured through the enzymatic breakdown of starch, resulting in a unique molecular structure that combines the benefits of both simple and complex carbohydrates.

This structure allows HBCD to empty quickly from the stomach and be easily absorbed in the small intestine, providing an immediate source of glucose for the muscles.

The rapid absorption of HBCD minimizes the possibility of gastrointestinal discomfort sometimes associated with other fast-digesting carbohydrates.

One of the main benefits of HBCD is its ability to quickly replenish glycogen stores after intense exercise.

During high-intensity training, muscle glycogen stores are depleted, leading to fatigue and decreased performance.

As a fast-digesting carbohydrate source, HBCD can quickly restore these glycogen levels, facilitating faster recovery and preparing the muscles for future training sessions.

In addition to its glycogen-replenishing capabilities, HBCD can also help improve performance during exercise.

By providing a rapid source of energy, HBCD can help maintain stable blood glucose levels, reducing fatigue and improving endurance.

This is particularly beneficial for athletes engaging in prolonged or high-intensity training.

HBCD also has a positive impact on insulin secretion.

The rapid digestion and absorption of HBCD cause an increase in insulin levels, an anabolic hormone that promotes the uptake of glucose and amino acids into muscle cells.

This effect can enhance muscle protein synthesis and reduce muscle breakdown, supporting muscle growth and recovery.

To maximize the benefits of HBCD, it is recommended to consume it immediately after exercise when muscles are most receptive to glucose uptake and glycogen synthesis.

HBCD can be combined with fast-absorbing proteins, such as whey, to provide an optimal mix of carbohydrates and essential amino acids for post-workout recovery.

In terms of dosage, the amount of HBCD needed can vary based on the type, duration, and intensity of exercise, as well as the athlete's weight and goals.

Generally, a dose of 30-60 grams of HBCD after exercise is recommended, though individual needs may vary.

HBCD is considered safe and well-tolerated by most people; however, as with any supplement, it is important to follow dosing recommendations and consider individual needs and potential interactions with other supplements or medications.

51

Arnold Schwarzenegger.

Born on July 30, 1947, in Thal, Austria, he is one of the most iconic and multifaceted figures in bodybuilding, cinema, and politics.

His career began in bodybuilding, where he quickly stood out and became a legend in the sport.

Arnold won the Mr. Olympia title seven times (1970-1975, 1980), and is widely considered one of the greatest bodybuilders of all time.

His record of seven titles was only later surpassed by Lee Haney and Ronnie Coleman.

Arnold started his bodybuilding career at a young age.

At 18, he won the title of Mr. Junior Europe, and in 1967, he became the youngest man to win Mr. Universe at the age of 20.

This victory was the first of many in his rise in the bodybuilding world.

Schwarzenegger moved to the United States in 1968, where he continued to perfect his physique and compete professionally.

In addition to his Mr. Olympia titles, Arnold won several other prestigious bodybuilding contests, including Mr. Universe and Mr. World.

His impressive physique and charisma made him a prominent figure in bodybuilding and an ambassador of the sport worldwide.

His focus on symmetry, proportion, and muscle size set a new standard in professional bodybuilding.

Arnold not only excelled in bodybuilding but also became a world-renowned movie star.

His Hollywood career took off with the film "Hercules in New York" (1970), although his first major success came with "Conan the Barbarian" (1982).

His role in "The Terminator" (1984), directed by James Cameron, catapulted him to stardom and made him an international star.

The phrase "I'll be back" became a cultural icon.

Schwarzenegger continued to star in numerous successful films, including "Predator" (1987), "Total Recall" (1990), "Kindergarten Cop" (1990), and the "Terminator" series.

In addition to his film career, Arnold ventured into politics.

In 2003, he was elected Governor of California in a special recall election.

During his tenure as governor, which lasted until 2011, he focused on issues such as pension system reform, infrastructure, and renewable energy.

His leadership in the world's eighth-largest economy cemented his reputation as a serious and committed politician.

Arnold is also a successful entrepreneur and philanthropist, investing in real estate, various businesses, and advocating for physical education and wellness.

He founded the Arnold Sports Festival, one of the largest sports events in the world, featuring bodybuilding, weightlifting, and many other sports competitions.

Throughout his life, Arnold has received numerous awards and recognitions for his achievements in bodybuilding, film, and politics.

He has been honored with the Order of Merit of the Republic of Austria and has received multiple cinematic achievement awards, including a Golden Globe for Best Acting Debut in "Stay Hungry" (1976).

Arnold Schwarzenegger is also the author of several books, including his autobiography "Total Recall: My Unbelievably True Life Story" (2012), which details his life from his childhood in Austria to his career in bodybuilding, film, and politics.

52

Lee Haney.

Born on November 11, 1959, in Fairburn, Georgia, Lee Haney is one of the most successful and respected bodybuilders of all time.

Haney is especially known for his impressive achievement of winning the Mr. Olympia title eight consecutive times, from 1984 to 1991, a record he shares with Ronnie Coleman.

This accomplishment cemented his place in bodybuilding history and highlighted him for his incredible symmetry, muscle size, and focus on physical aesthetics.

From an early age, Lee Haney showed a great interest in sports and physical conditioning.

He began weight training in his teenage years and quickly excelled in local and regional competitions.

His dedication and talent led him to win the Mr. America title in 1979 and Mr. Universe in 1982, marking the beginning of his rise in the professional bodybuilding world.

Haney's professional bodybuilding career took off in 1983 when he competed in his first Mr. Olympia, finishing in third place.

The following year, in 1984, he won his first Mr. Olympia title, starting an unmatched streak of eight consecutive victories in this prestigious competition.

During his reign as Mr. Olympia, Haney was known for his ability to combine massive musculature with exceptional symmetry and proportion, setting a new standard in professional bodybuilding.

In addition to his success in bodybuilding competitions, Haney has excelled as a personal trainer and fitness advisor.

After retiring from competitive bodybuilding, he founded Lee Haney's Nutritional Support System, a company dedicated to providing nutritional supplements and fitness advice.

He has also worked as a personal trainer for celebrities and athletes, sharing his knowledge and experience in physical conditioning and nutrition.

Lee Haney has been a tireless advocate for fitness and overall health and has authored several books on bodybuilding and fitness, including "Totalee Awesome: A Complete Guide to Bodybuilding Success" and "Fit at Any Age: Exercise to Stimulate Not Annihilate."

His books and training programs have helped countless people achieve their fitness and health goals.

In recognition of his contributions to bodybuilding and fitness, Haney has received numerous awards and honors.

He was inducted into the IFBB (International Federation of Bodybuilding & Fitness) Hall of Fame and has been recognized for his philanthropic work, including his support of charitable organizations and his work with youth through mentorship and fitness programs.

Haney also served as chairman of the President's Council on Physical Fitness and Sports under President Bill Clinton's administration, where he promoted the importance of exercise and nutrition for the health and well-being of Americans.

In addition to his professional success, Lee Haney is known for his character and personal values, as he is a man of deep Christian faith and has spoken openly about how his beliefs have influenced his life and career.

He is married to Shirley Haney, and together they have two children, so his dedication to his family and community continues to inspire people of all ages to lead a healthy and active lifestyle.

53

Iris Kyle, born on August 22, 1974, in Benton Harbor, Michigan, is one of the most prominent and successful figures in the history of female bodybuilding.

With an impressive record of ten Ms. Olympia titles (2004, 2006-2014), Kyle is recognized as the most successful female bodybuilder of all time.

Her dominance in female bodybuilding is unparalleled, and her career has left an indelible mark on the sport.

Kyle began her bodybuilding career in the 1990s, motivated by her passion for fitness and muscle development.

Before entering the bodybuilding world, Kyle was an outstanding athlete in basketball, track, and field during her youth.

However, her interest in bodybuilding grew when she started working at a gym and was encouraged to compete by her friends and colleagues.

Her first major victory came in 1994 when she won the Ms. Orange County title.

This triumph was followed by victories in other regional and national competitions, quickly establishing her as a dominant force in female bodybuilding.

In 1998, Kyle earned her professional card by winning the National Physique Committee (NPC) USA Bodybuilding Championship, which allowed her to compete professionally in the International Federation of Bodybuilding & Fitness (IFBB).

Kyle's rise in the professional bodybuilding world was meteoric.

She won her first Ms. Olympia title in 2004 and then dominated the competition for a decade, amassing a total of ten Ms. Olympia titles.

In addition to her Ms. Olympia titles, Kyle also won seven Ms. International titles, another of the most prestigious competitions in female bodybuilding, further solidifying her legacy in the sport.

Kyle is known for her impressive physique, which combines massive musculature with exceptional definition and symmetry.

Her ability to present such a balanced and aesthetically pleasing physique in every competition made her stand out among her peers and allowed her to maintain her dominance in female bodybuilding for many years.

Beyond her competitive success, Kyle has been an ambassador for female bodybuilding and has worked to promote the sport and support future generations of bodybuilders.

Throughout her career, she has been a source of inspiration and motivation for many women seeking to achieve excellence in bodybuilding.

Kyle has also ventured into the business and fitness world, launching her own line of supplements and training equipment.

Her focus on nutrition and training has benefited not only bodybuilders but also those looking to improve their overall health and fitness.

Throughout her career, Iris Kyle has received numerous recognitions and awards for her achievements in bodybuilding.

She has been inducted into the IFBB Hall of Fame and has been honored for her contributions to the sport.

Her legacy endures as a symbol of dedication, perseverance, and excellence in female bodybuilding.

54

Dexter Jackson, born on November 25, 1969, in Jacksonville, Florida, is one of the most successful and enduring bodybuilders in professional bodybuilding history.

Known as "The Blade" due to his impressive definition and physique, Jackson has left an indelible mark on the sport.

Throughout his career, he has set the record for the most victories in IFBB professional competitions, with over 29 wins, and has been a consistent and successful competitor for decades.

Dexter Jackson began his bodybuilding career at a relatively late age compared to other competitors, debuting in local competitions in the 1990s.

His first major victory came in 1992 when he won the NPC Southern States Championship.

From there, his career quickly took off, distinguished by his incredible consistency and ability to present himself in peak physical condition at every competition.

Jackson earned his professional card in 1998 and quickly began racking up victories on the IFBB professional circuit.

His first major professional victory was at the 2005 Arnold Classic, one of the most prestigious competitions in bodybuilding after the Mr. Olympia.

Dexter Jackson won the Arnold Classic five times (2005, 2006, 2008, 2013, and 2015), solidifying his reputation as one of the best bodybuilders of his generation.

The highlight of his career came in 2008 when he won the Mr. Olympia title.

This victory was particularly significant as it broke Jay Cutler's winning streak, who had won the title in 2006 and 2007.

Dexter Jackson's victory at the 2008 Mr. Olympia highlighted his ability to achieve and maintain exceptional physical condition and his skill to compete at the highest level.

In addition to his Mr. Olympia title, Jackson has been a constant competitor in this event, participating more than 20 times throughout his career.

His longevity and consistency in the sport are admirable, competing regularly in multiple competitions each year and always presenting himself in excellent shape.

Throughout his career, Jackson has been known for his incredible recovery ability and longevity.

Even as he aged, he continued to compete and win major competitions, which is rare in professional bodybuilding.

In 2015, at the age of 45, he won the Arnold Classic, proving that he could still compete at the highest level.

Jackson has also been an inspiring figure off the stage.

He has launched his own supplement line, Dexter Jackson Signature Series, and has been a mentor and coach to many young bodybuilders.

His work ethic, dedication, and focus on continuous improvement have inspired many both within and outside the bodybuilding world.

In terms of awards and recognitions, besides his Mr. Olympia title and his five Arnold Classic victories, Jackson has won multiple IFBB competitions, including the Grand Prix Australia, New Zealand Pro, Russian Grand Prix, and the Tampa Pro.

His record of more than 29 professional IFBB victories is a testament to his skill, consistency, and longevity in the sport.

55

Phil Heath.

His full name is Phillip Jerrod Heath, and he was born on December 18, 1979, in Seattle, Washington.

Heath won the prestigious Mr. Olympia title seven consecutive times, from 2011 to 2017, matching the feat of Arnold Schwarzenegger and only surpassed by Ronnie Coleman and Lee Haney, who each have eight titles.

Phil Heath began his athletic career as a basketball player at the University of Denver, where he received a sports scholarship.

However, his interest in bodybuilding grew during his college years, leading him to change direction and dedicate himself to weight training.

Heath made his bodybuilding debut in 2003 and quickly stood out, winning his first major title in 2005, the NPC USA Championships, where he earned his IFBB professional card.

Heath's professional career took off rapidly, distinguished by his ability to present an almost perfect physical condition on stage.

In 2006, he won his first professional contest, the Colorado Pro Championships, followed by the New York Pro Championships.

These initial successes established Heath as an emerging force in the bodybuilding world.

Heath continued to rise in the professional bodybuilding rankings, winning several important competitions before making his Mr. Olympia debut in 2008, where he finished in third place.

His constant improvement and determination led him to win his first Mr. Olympia title in 2011.

Over the next seven years, Heath dominated the competition, winning the Mr. Olympia title from 2011 to 2017.

His continuous success was due to his ability to consistently enhance his physique, presenting an exceptional combination of muscle mass, definition, and symmetry.

In addition to his Mr. Olympia victories, Heath has also won other prestigious competitions, including the Arnold Classic Europe and the Sheru Classic.

His meticulous focus on diet, training, and recovery has been a key part of his success, and his work ethic and dedication are widely recognized in the bodybuilding community.

Phil Heath is known by his nickname "The Gift" due to his superior genetics and exceptional muscle development.

His muscular development includes outstanding definition, especially in areas such as the arms, chest, and back, making him a benchmark for aesthetics and proportion in bodybuilding.

Off the stage, Heath has been a successful entrepreneur and an influential figure in the fitness industry.

He has launched his own line of supplements and sportswear and has been a spokesperson and ambassador for several major brands.

Additionally, he has appeared in numerous fitness magazines and participated in documentaries about bodybuilding, sharing his knowledge and experience with a global audience.

In terms of awards and recognitions, besides his seven Mr. Olympia titles, Heath has received numerous honors and trophies throughout his career.

56

Lenda Murray.

Born on February 22, 1962, in Detroit, Michigan, Murray won the Ms. Olympia title eight times, tying with Lee Haney and Ronnie Coleman for the most Olympia victories, placing her among the greatest in the sport.

Lenda Murray began her athletic career as a cheerleader and runner in college, excelling with her athletic physique and dedication to sports.

Her transition to bodybuilding began in the 1980s when she was inspired by watching the Ms. Olympia competition on television.

Murray then decided to pursue professional bodybuilding, and in 1985, she won her first major title, the NPC Michigan State Championships.

Her rise in bodybuilding was swift; in 1989, Murray won the NPC USA Championships, earning her professional card in the International Federation of Bodybuilding & Fitness (IFBB).

Her debut in Ms. Olympia was in 1990, and she not only competed but won the title on her first attempt, marking the beginning of an era of dominance in female bodybuilding.

Murray won the Ms. Olympia title six consecutive years, from 1990 to 1995, establishing herself as an unstoppable force in the sport.

After losing the title in 1996 and taking a break from competition, she made a strong comeback in 2002 to reclaim the Ms. Olympia title, winning again in 2002 and 2003.

Her ability to return and win after a hiatus demonstrated her incredible dedication and determination.

Murray's success in bodybuilding was due to her unique combination of muscle size, symmetry, and femininity.

Her physique was known for its elegant lines and balance, allowing her to stand out during a time when female bodybuilding was rapidly evolving.

Her stage presence and ability to connect with the audience also contributed to her success and popularity.

In addition to her Ms. Olympia titles, Murray has been recognized with numerous awards and honors throughout her career.

She has been inducted into the IFBB Hall of Fame and has received awards recognizing her contributions to the sport of bodybuilding.

Her impact goes beyond her victories, as she has been an advocate for female bodybuilding and has worked to promote and support future generations of bodybuilders.

After retiring from competition, Murray continued to be an influential figure in the fitness industry.

She has worked as a trainer, mentor, and fitness model, sharing her knowledge and experience with aspiring bodybuilders and fitness enthusiasts.

She has also been a frequent contributor to fitness magazines and has participated in bodybuilding events and expos worldwide.

Lenda Murray is known for her focus on overall health and wellness, promoting a balanced and healthy lifestyle.

She has used her platform to advocate for the importance of nutrition, proper training, and self-care, inspiring many people to follow in her footsteps and achieve their own fitness goals.

57

Jay Cutler.

His full name is Jason Isaac Cutler, and he was born on August 3, 1973, in Sterling, Massachusetts.

He is one of the most successful and popular bodybuilders in history, known for his impressive muscle size, definition, and symmetry.

Cutler won the prestigious Mr. Olympia title four times (2006, 2007, 2009, and 2010) and is recognized for being one of the few bodybuilders to regain the title after losing it, a rare achievement in professional bodybuilding.

Cutler became interested in bodybuilding at a young age, inspired by his older brother and iconic figures in the sport like Arnold Schwarzenegger.

He started weight training at 18 while working in his family's construction business.

His dedication and superior genetics quickly led him to excel in local and regional competitions.

In 1993, Cutler won his first major title, the NPC Iron Bodies Invitational.

This marked the beginning of his competitive bodybuilding career.

In 1996, he won the NPC Nationals, earning his IFBB (International Federation of Bodybuilding & Fitness) professional card.

His professional IFBB debut was in 1998, and although he didn't win immediately, he showed great potential and quickly became a standout competitor.

Cutler's rise in professional bodybuilding was meteoric.

In 2000, he won the Night of Champions and placed second at Mr. Olympia, behind the legendary Ronnie Coleman.

Over the next few years, Cutler and Coleman developed one of the most memorable rivalries in bodybuilding history.

Cutler placed second behind Coleman in the Mr. Olympia from 2001 to 2005, but his determination and constant improvement finally paid off.

In 2006, Jay Cutler managed to dethrone Ronnie Coleman, winning his first Mr. Olympia title.

Cutler repeated his victory in 2007, cementing his status as the best bodybuilder in the world at that time.

In 2008, he lost the title to Dexter Jackson but made history in 2009 by reclaiming the Mr. Olympia title, becoming the first bodybuilder to achieve this.

Cutler successfully defended his title in 2010, adding his fourth Mr. Olympia title.

In addition to his Mr. Olympia titles, Cutler won multiple major competitions throughout his career, including the Arnold Classic, the Ironman Pro Invitational, and the Pro Ironman.

His massive and aesthetic physique, combined with his charisma and professionalism, made him very popular among bodybuilding fans.

Off the stage, Jay Cutler has been a successful entrepreneur and an influential figure in the fitness industry.

He launched his own supplement line, Cutler Nutrition, and has participated in numerous seminars, expos, and bodybuilding events worldwide.

Cutler has also appeared in many fitness magazines and produced several training videos, sharing his knowledge and experience with a global audience.

Cutler is known for his meticulous and disciplined approach to training and nutrition; his training regimen includes heavy lifting and a strict diet, factors that significantly contributed to his success in bodybuilding.

58

Cory Everson.

Born on January 4, 1958, in Racine, Wisconsin, she is one of the most iconic and respected figures in the history of female bodybuilding.

Everson won the Ms. Olympia title six consecutive times, from 1984 to 1989, setting an impressive record and solidifying her place in the elite of female bodybuilding.

From an early age, Cory Everson showed an interest in sports and physical activity.

During her youth, she was an outstanding athlete in various sports, including gymnastics, track and field, and basketball.

She attended the University of Wisconsin-Madison, where she continued to participate in sports and graduated with a degree in physical education.

Everson began weight training to improve her athletic performance, which eventually led her to discover her passion for bodybuilding.

In 1980, she met Jeff Everson, a bodybuilder and trainer who would become her husband and coach.

With his support and guidance, Cory Everson began competing in bodybuilding and quickly stood out on the competitive stage.

Her competitive career took off in 1980 when she won the Ms. Mid America title.

This initial success was followed by victories in other competitions, culminating in her first win at the NPC National Championships in 1981.

Her talent and dedication to bodybuilding led her to earn her professional card in the IFBB.

In 1984, Cory Everson won her first Ms. Olympia title, the most prestigious female bodybuilding competition in the world.

This victory marked the beginning of her dominance in female bodybuilding.

Everson successfully defended her Ms. Olympia title six consecutive times, from 1984 to 1989, retiring undefeated after her sixth victory.

Her success in Ms. Olympia set a standard of excellence in the sport and made her a legendary figure in female bodybuilding.

Cory Everson's physique was characterized by balance, symmetry, and femininity, combined with well-developed and defined musculature.

Her focus on presentation and aesthetics made her stand out and win the appreciation of both judges and bodybuilding fans.

After retiring from competitive bodybuilding, Cory Everson continued to be an influential figure in the fitness and entertainment industry.

She appeared in several movies and TV shows, including "Double Impact" alongside Jean-Claude Van Damme and the TV series "Hercules: The Legendary Journeys."

She also hosted the fitness television show "BodyShaping" and later "Gotta Sweat."

Everson has also distinguished herself as an author and entrepreneur.

She has written several books on fitness and bodybuilding, sharing her knowledge and experience with a broader audience.

Her focus on overall health and wellness has inspired many people to adopt a healthier and more active lifestyle.

Throughout her career, Cory Everson has received numerous awards and recognitions for her achievements in bodybuilding and her contribution to fitness.

She has been inducted into the IFBB Hall of Fame and has received awards recognizing her influence and leadership in the sport.

59

Franco Columbu.

Born on August 7, 1941, in Ollolai, Sardinia, Italy, and passed away on August 30, 2019, in San Teodoro, Sardinia, he was one of the most respected and multifaceted figures in the world of bodybuilding and strength athletics.

In addition to his notable achievements in bodybuilding, including two Mr. Olympia titles (1976 and 1981), Columbu was known for his incredible strength and ability to compete at the highest level in various strength disciplines.

Columbu began his athletic career as a boxer and weightlifter before transitioning to bodybuilding.

His talent and natural strength quickly led him to stand out in the bodybuilding arena.

In the 1960s, he moved to Munich, Germany, where he met Arnold Schwarzenegger.

The two became close friends and training partners, and together they emigrated to the United States to pursue their careers in bodybuilding.

Franco Columbu won numerous titles in bodybuilding competitions before reaching the pinnacle of his career with his victories in Mr. Olympia.

He won Mr. Europe in 1970 and Mr. World in 1971.

His compact, dense, and extremely defined physique made him stand out in a sport dominated by much taller athletes.

In 1976, Columbu won his first Mr. Olympia title, and in 1981, after recovering from a severe leg injury sustained during the World's Strongest Man competition in 1977, he won his second Mr. Olympia title.

This victory in 1981 was particularly significant as it marked his triumphant return to the sport after an injury that many thought would end his career.

In addition to his success in bodybuilding, Columbu was known for his incredible strength.

He had an impressive list of strength achievements, including a personal record deadlift of 340 kg (750 pounds), a squat of 297 kg (655 pounds), and a bench press of 238 kg (525 pounds).

These feats of strength were remarkable, especially considering his height of 5 feet 5 inches (1.65 meters).

Franco Columbu also had a successful career as an actor and personal trainer.

He appeared in several films, often alongside his friend Arnold Schwarzenegger.

Some of his most notable appearances include roles in "Conan the Barbarian" and "The Terminator."

Additionally, he worked as a trainer and fitness advisor, helping numerous clients achieve their health and fitness goals.

Columbu was also a successful chiropractor, having graduated from the Cleveland Chiropractic College in Los Angeles.

He combined his knowledge of the human body and his experience in strength training to provide comprehensive treatments and health advice to his patients.

Throughout his career, Franco Columbu received numerous awards and recognitions for his achievements in bodybuilding and strength athletics.

He was inducted into the IFBB Hall of Fame and is remembered as one of the strongest and most complete bodybuilders of all time.

Columbu also published several books on bodybuilding and fitness, sharing his knowledge and experience with a wider audience.

His books, which include "Coming on Strong" and "Weight Training and Bodybuilding: A Complete Guide for Young Athletes," are valuable resources for those interested in bodybuilding and strength training.

60

Rich Gaspari.

Born on May 16, 1963, in New Brunswick, New Jersey, he is especially known for his impressive muscle definition and vascularity, as well as his innovations in training and nutrition.

Gaspari left an indelible mark on the sport and later became a successful entrepreneur in the nutritional supplement industry.

Gaspari began his bodybuilding career at a young age and quickly stood out for his dedication and ability to achieve a level of muscle definition that few could match.

In 1984, he earned his IFBB professional card by winning the NPC National Championships.

His rise in professional bodybuilding was swift, and he soon became one of the top contenders in the world's most prestigious competitions.

In 1986, Gaspari made his debut at Mr. Olympia, where he surprised many by finishing in second place, just behind the legendary Lee Haney.

This result marked the beginning of an impressive career in which Gaspari established himself as one of the best bodybuilders of his era.

He finished second at Mr. Olympia three consecutive times (1986, 1987, and 1988), demonstrating his consistency and ability to compete at the highest level.

In 1989, Rich Gaspari made history by becoming the first winner of the Arnold Classic, one of the most prestigious competitions in professional bodybuilding.

His victory at the Arnold Classic not only solidified his status as a bodybuilding legend but also underscored his ability to achieve an unmatched level of definition and vascularity.

Gaspari was a pioneer in training and diet techniques that focused on achieving extreme definition, influencing future generations of bodybuilders.

In addition to his competitive success, Gaspari has been an innovator in the nutritional supplement industry.

In 1998, he founded Gaspari Nutrition, a company that has become one of the leading brands in sports supplements.

The company has developed a wide range of products designed to enhance athletic performance, recovery, and overall health.

His expertise and knowledge in nutrition and training have been instrumental in the success of his company.

Rich Gaspari has also been a prolific author and motivational speaker.

He has written several books on bodybuilding and fitness, sharing his experience and advice with a global audience.

His book "51 Days No Excuses" is a comprehensive training and nutrition plan designed to help people transform their physique and improve their health.

Throughout his career, Gaspari has received numerous awards and recognitions for his contributions to bodybuilding and the fitness industry.

He has been inducted into the IFBB Hall of Fame and has been honored for his influence and leadership in the sport.

His legacy includes not only his competitive achievements but also his lasting impact on sports nutrition and training.

Gaspari is known for his work ethic and dedication, both in bodybuilding and business.

His ability to reinvent and adapt over the years has been a source of inspiration for many.

61

Frank Zane.

Born on June 28, 1942, in Kingston, Pennsylvania, he won the Mr. Olympia title three consecutive times, from 1977 to 1979, and is known for his focus on aesthetics and symmetry, in contrast to the predominant focus on sheer muscle mass.

His physique was characterized by impeccable proportion, definition, and elegant lines, making him a pioneer in the realm of aesthetic bodybuilding.

Frank Zane began his bodybuilding career at a young age and quickly stood out for his dedication and ability to achieve an aesthetically perfect physique.

He graduated from Wilkes University with a bachelor's degree in science and later earned a master's degree in experimental psychology from California State University, San Bernardino, allowing him to combine his academic knowledge with his passion for bodybuilding.

Zane competed in his first bodybuilding competition in 1961 and won Mr. Pennsylvania in 1963.

Throughout the 1960s and early 1970s, he continued to accumulate titles and recognition in the bodybuilding community.

In 1968, he achieved one of his first major victories by winning the NABBA Mr. Universe, and in 1970, he won the IFBB Mr. America title.

The highlight of Zane's career came in 1977 when he won his first Mr. Olympia title, the most prestigious bodybuilding contest in the world.

His victory was significant because it broke the prevailing trend towards massive physiques and demonstrated that a focus on symmetry, proportion, and aesthetics could be equally victorious.

Zane successfully defended his Mr. Olympia title in 1978 and 1979, establishing himself as one of the great champions in bodybuilding.

Zane's physique was distinguished by its perfect proportion, narrow waist, and exceptional muscle definition.

His meticulous focus on diet, training, and stage presentation made him a role model for those seeking an aesthetically pleasing physique.

His nickname, "The Chemist," stems from his deep knowledge of nutrition and supplementation, as well as his scientific approach to competition preparation.

In addition to his Mr. Olympia titles, Zane won other prestigious bodybuilding contests, including Mr. Universe and Mr. America.

Throughout his career, he received numerous awards and recognitions for his achievements and contributions to the sport of bodybuilding.

After retiring from competition, Frank Zane continued to be an influential figure in the fitness industry.

He opened his own gym and training center, Zane Experience, where he offered personalized training programs and advice to bodybuilders and fitness enthusiasts.

He also wrote several books on bodybuilding and fitness, including "The Zane Way to a Beautiful Body" and "Frank Zane: Mind, Body, Spirit," sharing his knowledge and experience with a wider audience.

Zane has been a frequent contributor to fitness magazines and has participated in seminars and bodybuilding events worldwide.

His focus on aesthetics and symmetry has influenced generations of bodybuilders and helped popularize a more balanced and harmonious approach to physical development.

62

Dorian Yates.

Born on April 19, 1962, in Hurley, England, he won the Mr. Olympia title six consecutive times, from 1992 to 1997, and is renowned for his massive physique and intense approach to training and nutrition.

Yates grew up in Birmingham, England, and developed an interest in bodybuilding at a relatively young age.

Despite a youth marked by challenges, including a period in a juvenile detention center, Yates channeled his energy into bodybuilding.

He began serious training in the early 1980s and quickly showed exceptional talent for developing muscle mass and definition.

Yates' career took off when he won the National Amateur Body-Builders' Association (NABBA) British Championship in 1986.

This victory catapulted him onto the international stage, and in 1990, he won the International Federation of Bodybuilding & Fitness (IFBB) British Championship, earning his professional card.

Yates made his Mr. Olympia debut in 1991, where he surprised many by finishing in second place behind Lee Haney.

His impressive physique, characterized by massive size, extreme definition, and symmetry, quickly established him as a serious contender for the title.

In 1992, Yates won his first Mr. Olympia title, starting a six-year reign at the pinnacle of professional bodybuilding.

He successfully defended his title each year until 1997, when he retired due to a series of severe injuries.

Dorian Yates revolutionized bodybuilding with his unique approach to training, known as "Heavy Duty."

This method, developed in collaboration with bodybuilder Mike Mentzer, focused on brief but extremely intense workouts, with an emphasis on reaching muscle failure in each set.

Yates trained with very heavy weights and performed few repetitions, allowing him to develop impressive muscle mass and exceptional density.

In addition to his training approach, Yates was also known for his rigorous attention to nutrition and supplementation.

He followed a strict diet, rich in protein and adjusted to optimize muscle growth and definition.

His dedication to every aspect of bodybuilding made him a pioneer and a source of inspiration for many in the sport.

Throughout his career, Yates won numerous awards and received many recognitions for his achievements.

He was inducted into the IFBB Hall of Fame and has been honored for his contribution to the sport of bodybuilding.

After retiring from competition, Dorian Yates has continued to be an influential figure in the world of fitness and bodybuilding.

He founded Dorian Yates Nutrition, a supplement company offering products designed to enhance performance and recovery.

He has also written several books and produced training videos, sharing his knowledge and experience with a global audience.

Yates has been a motivational speaker and has participated in numerous seminars and bodybuilding events worldwide.

63

Lou Ferrigno.

Born on November 9, 1951, in Brooklyn, New York, he is an iconic figure in both the world of bodybuilding and the entertainment industry.

Although best known for his role in the television series "The Incredible Hulk," Ferrigno had a distinguished career in bodybuilding, winning titles such as Mr. Universe.

From a young age, Ferrigno faced significant challenges, including partial hearing loss due to an ear infection during his childhood; however, this did not deter him from pursuing his dreams.

Inspired by bodybuilders like Steve Reeves and the legendary Arnold Schwarzenegger, Ferrigno began weight training at an early age and quickly excelled in amateur bodybuilding.

Ferrigno won his first major bodybuilding title in 1971 when he was crowned champion at the IFBB Mr. America.

The following year, in 1972, he won the Mr. Universe title, a feat he repeated in 1973.

These victories cemented his status as one of the most promising bodybuilders of his generation.

Throughout the 1970s, Ferrigno continued competing and had a notable rivalry with Arnold Schwarzenegger.

This rivalry was immortalized in the documentary "Pumping Iron" (1977), which provided a behind-the-scenes look at the world of bodybuilding and helped popularize the sport.

Although Ferrigno did not win the Mr. Olympia during this period, his impressive size and musculature made him a formidable competitor.

In addition to his bodybuilding career, Ferrigno became a cultural icon when he was cast as the Hulk in the television series "The Incredible Hulk" (1977-1982).

His portrayal of the character, combined with his impressive physique, made him an international star and opened the door to an acting career.

He continued to play the Hulk in various TV movies and related projects over the years.

Following his success on television, Ferrigno continued his career in entertainment and fitness.

He appeared in several movies, TV shows, and theatrical productions, always leveraging his physique and stage presence.

He also competed in the World's Strongest Man in 1977, showcasing his strength and athletic ability.

In the 1990s, Ferrigno returned to competitive bodybuilding.

He competed in the Mr. Olympia in 1992 and 1993, impressing many with his ability to maintain a competitive physique at an older age.

Although he did not win, his return to the stage demonstrated his dedication and passion for bodybuilding.

Ferrigno has also been a successful entrepreneur and fitness advocate.

He opened several gyms and launched his own line of supplements and fitness equipment.

Additionally, he has worked as a personal trainer and fitness consultant, helping countless individuals achieve their health and fitness goals.

He was inducted into the IFBB Hall of Fame and has been honored with various awards for his work as an actor and bodybuilder.

Notably, he has been an advocate for hearing loss awareness and has worked to support people with hearing disabilities.

64

Kevin Levrone.

Born on July 16, 1964, in Baltimore, Maryland, he is known as "The Maryland Muscle Machine."

Levrone has won more than 20 IFBB professional competitions and is famous for his ability to achieve competition-level conditioning in record time.

Levrone became interested in bodybuilding in his youth, inspired by the success of bodybuilders like Arnold Schwarzenegger and Lee Haney.

His competitive career took off in 1991 when he won the NPC Nationals, earning his IFBB professional card.

His impressive professional debut came in 1992 when he won the prestigious Arnold Classic.

This victory marked the beginning of a stellar career in bodybuilding.

Throughout his career, Levrone was known for his massive physique, symmetry, and ability to present exceptional conditioning at every competition.

He competed in Mr. Olympia numerous times, finishing second on four occasions (1992, 1995, 2000, and 2002), always on the verge of capturing bodybuilding's most prestigious title.

Although he never won Mr. Olympia, his consistency and competitive level placed him among the best bodybuilders of his era.

Levrone won the Arnold Classic twice (1994 and 1996), cementing his reputation as one of the most successful bodybuilders of the 1990s.

He also won several other major competitions, including the Grand Prix England, the San Francisco Pro Invitational, and the Night of Champions.

His total of over 20 professional victories in the IFBB is a testament to his dedication and skill in bodybuilding.

One of Kevin Levrone's most notable characteristics was his ability to "hibernate" during the off-season and then transform his physique in record time for competitions.

This ability to achieve a world-class physique in short preparation periods is something that few bodybuilders have been able to match.

Levrone often took long breaks from intense training, only to return and compete at the highest level with minimal prior preparation.

In addition to his success in bodybuilding, Levrone has also ventured into music and acting.

He is a talented singer and has released several rock singles.

His passion for music has been an integral part of his life outside of bodybuilding, and he has performed at various events and concerts.

After retiring from competitive bodybuilding in the early 2000s, Levrone remained active in the fitness and bodybuilding industry.

He founded his own supplement line, Levrone Signature Series, and has worked as a trainer and mentor for aspiring bodybuilders and fitness enthusiasts.

His knowledge and experience in training and nutrition have been valuable to many athletes worldwide.

In 2016, Levrone surprised the bodybuilding world by announcing his return to Mr. Olympia after more than a decade away from competition.

Although he did not win, his comeback was impressive and showcased his ability to compete at the highest level even after a long absence.

This return further strengthened his legacy as one of the greats in bodybuilding.

65

Omega-3 fatty acids, which are abundant in fish and fish oil supplements, have been shown to have numerous health benefits, including the prevention of muscle protein degradation during intense training.

Omega-3s are essential fatty acids, meaning the body cannot produce them on its own and they must be obtained through diet or supplementation.

Omega-3s are primarily composed of eicosapentaenoic acid (EPA) and docosahexaenoic acid (DHA), which are the most beneficial types for health.

These fatty acids have potent anti-inflammatory properties, which play a crucial role in muscle protection and recovery.

During intense training, the body can experience an increase in inflammation and oxidative stress, which can lead to muscle protein degradation and a higher risk of injury.

Supplementation with omega-3s can help mitigate these negative effects by reducing inflammation and muscle damage.

Studies have shown that omega-3s can increase muscle protein synthesis, improve muscle function, and reduce muscle degradation.

This is due to their ability to influence cellular signaling pathways involved in inflammation and protein metabolism.

In addition to their anti-inflammatory effects, omega-3s also improve insulin sensitivity, which is beneficial for nutrient absorption in muscle cells.

Better insulin sensitivity facilitates the delivery of amino acids and glucose to the muscles, promoting recovery and muscle growth.

Omega-3 consumption has also been associated with improved blood circulation, which can enhance the delivery of oxygen and nutrients to the muscles during exercise, thus helping to improve performance and recovery.

This is especially important for athletes and those who engage in intense training regularly.

The recommended dosage of omega-3 varies, but many experts suggest a daily intake of at least 1-2 grams of combined EPA and DHA.

This can be achieved through a diet rich in fatty fish such as salmon, mackerel, and sardines, as well as through high-quality fish oil supplements.

66

Maintaining optimal electrolyte levels is crucial for muscle contraction and proper nerve function.

Electrolytes such as calcium, magnesium, sodium, and potassium play vital roles in numerous bodily functions, including the regulation of fluid balance, nerve impulse transmission, and muscle contraction.

Calcium is essential for muscle contraction and nerve transmission.

It is fundamental for the release of neurotransmitters and the activation of contractile proteins in muscles.

A deficiency in calcium can lead to muscle cramps, weakness, and coordination problems.

Magnesium is also crucial for muscle and nerve function.

It acts as a cofactor in over 300 enzymatic reactions in the body, including those involved in energy production and protein synthesis.

Magnesium helps regulate calcium and potassium levels in cells, which is essential for maintaining nerve and muscle function.

Magnesium deficiency can cause muscle cramps, fatigue, and muscle spasms.

Sodium is a key electrolyte that helps maintain fluid balance in the body and is essential for nerve and muscle function.

Sodium facilitates the transmission of nerve impulses and muscle contraction.

It is especially important during exercise, as it is lost through sweat.

The lack of sodium can lead to dehydration, muscle cramps, and electrolyte imbalance.

Potassium is another vital electrolyte crucial for muscle and nerve function.

It helps maintain fluid and electrolyte balance in cells and is necessary for muscle contraction and nerve function.

Potassium also helps counteract the effects of sodium and can help maintain healthy blood pressure levels.

A deficiency in potassium can cause muscle weakness, cramps, and irregular heart rhythms.

To ensure optimal levels of these electrolytes, it is important to include a variety of foods rich in these nutrients in your diet.

Brightly colored fruits and vegetables are excellent sources of electrolytes.

For example, leafy greens like spinach and kale are rich in calcium and magnesium.

Bananas, oranges, and potatoes are good sources of potassium.

Dairy products and nuts are also rich in calcium and magnesium.

In addition to fruits and vegetables, consuming whole and unprocessed foods can help maintain an adequate electrolyte balance.

Avoiding excessive consumption of processed foods, which are often high in sodium but low in other electrolytes, is crucial for maintaining balance.

Proper hydration is also important for electrolyte balance.

Drinking enough water helps maintain blood volume and fluid balance, which is essential for the proper function of electrolytes.

67

**Gut bacteria, also known as gut microbiota,
play a crucial role in digesting the foods you eat.**

These bacteria help break down nutrients, synthesize essential vitamins, and contribute to protection against pathogens.

Maintaining a healthy gut is fundamental for good digestion, proper immune function, and overall well-being.

The gut microbiota is composed of trillions of microorganisms, including bacteria, viruses, and fungi, that primarily reside in the large intestine.

These bacteria ferment indigestible dietary fibers and other food components, producing short-chain fatty acids (SCFAs) such as butyrate, which serve as an energy source for colon cells and have anti-inflammatory effects.

To maintain gut health, it is important to consume probiotics, which are live microorganisms that can provide health benefits when consumed in adequate amounts.

Probiotics help maintain the balance of the gut microbiota, improving digestion and strengthening the immune system.

Some of the most common sources of probiotics include fermented foods such as yogurt, kefir, sauerkraut, kimchi, miso, and tempeh.

Yogurt is a fermented dairy product that contains live cultures of beneficial bacteria, such as Lactobacillus and Bifidobacterium.

These probiotics can improve lactose digestion, reduce intestinal inflammation, and enhance overall gut health.

Kefir is another fermented dairy beverage that contains a greater variety of probiotic strains compared to yogurt, which can provide additional benefits for gut health.

In addition to consuming probiotics, it is important to include prebiotics in your diet.

Prebiotics are indigestible fibers that act as food for beneficial bacteria in the gut.

Foods rich in prebiotics include bananas, asparagus, onions, garlic, artichokes, and whole grains.

The combination of probiotics and prebiotics can help promote a healthy and balanced gut microbiome.

A healthy gut microbiome not only improves digestion but also has a positive impact on mental and emotional health.

There is a connection between the gut and the brain known as the gut-brain axis.

Gut bacteria produce neurotransmitters and other compounds that can influence mood, stress, and cognitive function.

An imbalance in the gut microbiota has been associated with disorders such as anxiety, depression, and irritable bowel syndrome (IBS).

In addition to consuming foods rich in probiotics and prebiotics, other habits can contribute to gut health.

Maintaining a balanced, fiber-rich diet, drinking enough water, exercising regularly, and avoiding excessive use of antibiotics, which can disrupt the balance of gut microbiota, are important practices.

68

For every gram of glycogen your cells absorb, they take in approximately three grams of water.

Glycogen is a form of carbohydrate storage in the body, primarily stored in the liver and muscles.

When you consume carbohydrates, they break down into glucose, which can then be used immediately by the cells for energy or stored as glycogen for future use.

The process of storing glycogen in muscle and liver cells is closely related to water retention.

Each molecule of glycogen is associated with a significant amount of water, typically three to four grams of water per gram of glycogen.

This relationship is due to the hydrophilic nature of glycogen, which attracts and retains water within the cells.

This phenomenon has several important implications for body physiology and athletic performance.

First, cellular hydration is essential for optimal metabolic function.

Water is necessary for the biochemical reactions that occur during the synthesis and breakdown of glycogen.

Additionally, adequate hydration helps maintain cellular turgor, which is crucial for the function and integrity of muscle cells.

The relationship between glycogen and water also explains why low-carb diets can result in rapid initial weight loss.

When carbohydrate intake is reduced, the body depletes its glycogen stores, leading to a significant loss of associated water.

This water loss can be temporary and does not reflect a true loss of body fat.

For athletes and people engaging in intense physical activities, maintaining adequate glycogen levels is crucial for performance.

Muscle glycogen is a key energy source during high-intensity and endurance exercise.

Glycogen depletion can lead to fatigue and a decrease in performance.

Therefore, replenishing glycogen through adequate carbohydrate intake is essential for recovery and preparation for the next training session or competition.

Carbohydrate loading is a strategy used by athletes to maximize glycogen stores before a competition.

This strategy involves increasing carbohydrate intake several days before the event, along with a reduction in training intensity, to saturate glycogen stores in the muscles.

This practice not only increases energy reserves but also improves cellular hydration due to the water retention associated with glycogen.

Caffeine is widely recognized as one of the best stimulants for increasing energy and improving performance.

It is a natural compound found in various plants, such as coffee beans, tea leaves, and cacao seeds.

Caffeine acts as a central nervous system stimulant, making it a popular substance for enhancing alertness, concentration, and physical performance.

One of the primary ways caffeine improves performance is through its ability to block adenosine receptors in the brain.

Adenosine is a neurotransmitter that promotes sleep and relaxation.

By blocking these receptors, caffeine reduces the sensation of fatigue and increases wakefulness, resulting in a greater sense of energy and alertness.

In terms of physical performance, caffeine has several well-documented benefits.

It can improve aerobic endurance, muscle strength, and anaerobic capacity.

Studies have shown that caffeine can increase fat oxidation during exercise, which conserves glycogen stores and prolongs physical effort.

This is especially beneficial for endurance athletes, such as runners and cyclists.

Caffeine can also enhance performance in high-intensity, short-duration activities, such as weightlifting and sprints.

It improves muscle contraction by increasing the release of calcium in muscle cells and enhancing the transmission of nerve impulses.

Additionally, caffeine can reduce the perception of effort, allowing athletes to work harder and longer without feeling the same level of fatigue.

The effective dose of caffeine for performance enhancement varies by individual but generally falls within the range of 3 to 6 milligrams per kilogram of body weight.

This dose can be consumed in the form of coffee, tea, caffeine supplements, or energy drinks.

It is important to note that excessive caffeine consumption can lead to negative side effects such as anxiety, insomnia, heart palpitations, and gastrointestinal discomfort.

Besides its benefits for physical performance, caffeine can also improve cognitive performance.

It enhances attention, memory, and information processing capabilities.

These effects are useful not only for athletes but also for individuals who need to stay alert and focused for extended periods, such as students and professionals.

Caffeine has a relatively good safety profile when consumed in moderate doses.

However, it is important for individuals to be aware of their personal tolerance and potential side effects.

Some people may be more sensitive to caffeine and experience adverse effects even at lower doses.

70

Epsom salt baths, also known as Epsom salt baths, are a popular practice for facilitating recovery from intense training and reducing muscle pain.

Epsom salt is a crystalline form of magnesium sulfate, a mineral that has several health benefits when absorbed through the skin.

One of the main benefits of Epsom salt baths is their ability to reduce muscle pain and inflammation.

Magnesium, a key component of Epsom salt, plays a crucial role in muscle and nerve function.

Magnesium has been shown to help relax muscles, reduce cramps, and relieve muscle tension.

By soaking in an Epsom salt bath, magnesium can be absorbed through the skin, helping to replenish the body's levels of this mineral and alleviate muscle pain.

In addition to its relaxing properties, Epsom salt baths can help reduce inflammation and swelling.

Magnesium sulfate has anti-inflammatory effects that can be beneficial for people suffering from muscle and joint pain after intense exercise.

Soaking in an Epsom salt bath can help decrease inflammation and speed up recovery.

Epsom salt baths can also improve blood circulation.

The heat of the bathwater combined with magnesium can help dilate blood vessels, improving blood flow to muscles and tissues.

Improved circulation can facilitate the removal of toxins and metabolic waste products, such as lactic acid, that accumulate during exercise and contribute to muscle pain.

Another benefit of Epsom salt baths is their ability to promote relaxation and reduce stress.

Magnesium is known for its calming effect on the nervous system, and a warm Epsom salt bath can help alleviate stress and anxiety.

Muscle and mental relaxation can contribute to faster recovery and better sleep quality, both of which are important for recovery after exercise.

To prepare an Epsom salt bath, it is recommended to dissolve around 2 cups (approximately 475 grams) of Epsom salt in a bathtub filled with warm water.

Soaking in the bath for about 20-30 minutes allows the magnesium to be absorbed through the skin.

It is important to stay well-hydrated before and after the bath to avoid dehydration.

Although Epsom salt baths are generally safe, it is important for people with pre-existing health conditions, such as kidney or cardiovascular diseases, to consult a doctor before using them regularly.

Additionally, people with sensitive skin or skin conditions should exercise caution, as magnesium sulfate can irritate the skin in some cases.

71

Contrast showers, which alternate between periods of hot and cold water, are a technique used to increase blood flow after a workout and accelerate recovery.

This method typically involves 3 minutes of hot water followed by 3 minutes of cold water, repeating this cycle several times.

The principle behind contrast showers is based on the vasodilation and vasoconstriction of blood vessels.

Hot water causes the blood vessels to dilate (vasodilation), increasing blood flow to the muscles and superficial tissues.

This helps supply essential oxygen and nutrients while removing metabolic waste products like lactic acid, which accumulate during exercise.

Conversely, cold water causes the blood vessels to constrict (vasoconstriction), which helps reduce inflammation and edema.

By alternating between hot and cold water, a kind of "pumping" effect is created that improves blood and lymphatic circulation, promoting faster and more efficient recovery.

Contrast showers also have additional benefits, including reducing muscle pain and stiffness.

The change in temperatures can relieve muscle tension and provide a sense of well-being.

Additionally, cold water has an analgesic effect that can decrease the perception of pain after an intense workout.

This method is used by many athletes and trainers as part of their recovery programs.

Contrast showers not only improve circulation and waste elimination but can also have positive effects on the immune system.

By improving circulation, the body's immune response can be enhanced, helping to prevent infections and speed up the healing of minor injuries.

To perform a contrast shower, it is recommended to start with hot water for 3 minutes, followed by cold water for 3 minutes.

This cycle can be repeated 3 to 4 times.

It is important to ensure that the water is not too hot to avoid burns, nor too cold to avoid thermal shock, especially for individuals with pre-existing cardiovascular conditions.

In addition to showers, the contrast technique can also be applied using alternating baths in hot and cold water, particularly for the extremities.

This can be useful for athletes who want to focus recovery on specific areas such as the legs or arms.

Drinking alcohol can have negative effects on productivity and physical performance, primarily due to its impact on hormone levels, specifically the increase of estrogen and the decrease of testosterone.

These hormonal changes can affect body composition, physical performance, and muscle recovery.

Alcohol interferes with hormonal function in several ways. Firstly, alcohol consumption can increase estrogen levels in the body.

Estrogen is a hormone that, although important in both sexes, can lead to fat accumulation and hinder muscle development when in excess.

Alcohol can increase the activity of the enzyme aromatase, which converts testosterone into estrogen, thereby raising estrogen levels and lowering testosterone levels.

Testosterone is a crucial hormone for muscle development, strength, and recovery.

It is known for its role in protein synthesis and promoting an anabolic environment in the body.

The reduction of testosterone levels due to alcohol consumption can have several negative effects, including a decrease in muscle mass, an increase in fat accumulation, and a reduction in recovery capacity after exercise.

In addition to hormonal changes, alcohol has other adverse effects that can impact performance and overall health.

Alcohol dehydrates the body, which can negatively affect muscle function and recovery.

Dehydration can lead to muscle cramps, fatigue, and an increased risk of injury.

It can also disrupt the electrolyte balance, which is crucial for muscle contraction and nerve function.

Alcohol can also negatively affect sleep quality.

Although some people believe alcohol helps them fall asleep, it can actually disrupt the deep and REM sleep phases, resulting in lower quality sleep and insufficient recovery.

Sleep is essential for muscle recovery and tissue regeneration, and sleep disruption can lead to decreased performance and recovery capacity.

Additionally, alcohol can affect muscle protein synthesis, which is the process by which the body repairs and builds new muscle fibers after exercise.

Alcohol can inhibit the signaling pathways that regulate protein synthesis, resulting in slower and less efficient recovery.

Excessive alcohol consumption can also have long-term negative effects on cardiovascular health, liver function, and metabolism.

The liver, which is responsible for metabolizing alcohol, can become damaged over time due to excessive consumption, affecting its ability to detoxify the body and regulate hormone levels.

73

The myth that the body can only absorb 30 grams of protein per meal has been extensively debated in the fields of nutrition and fitness.

The reality is that the body is capable of digesting and absorbing more than 30 grams of protein in a single intake.

The protein we consume through food is broken down in our digestive tract into amino acids or di- and tripeptides, which are small chains of amino acids.

The absorption of these amino acids and peptides occurs in the small intestine through different transporters.

One of these transporters is PEPT1, which is specific for the absorption of di- and tripeptides, allowing for faster absorption compared to free amino acids, which rely on sodium-dependent transporters.

Gastric emptying, which is the process of emptying the stomach contents into the small intestine, also plays a crucial role in the rate of amino acid absorption.

Factors such as the fat content in the meal, the nature of the foods (solid versus liquid), and the volume of the intake can slow down gastric emptying and, therefore, affect the rate of nutrient absorption.

It's common for athletes to become obsessed with the speed of post-workout protein intake due to the concept of the anabolic window, which is the post-workout period when the body is believed to be more receptive to muscle protein synthesis.

However, this concept has been reconsidered, and it is now understood that protein synthesis can be effectively stimulated over a longer period.

A critical point that is often confused is the difference between "absorbing" and "utilizing."

While the body can absorb large amounts of protein in a single meal, it doesn't necessarily use all that protein immediately for muscle protein synthesis.

The body's ability to use amino acids for muscle protein synthesis depends on various factors, including training status, total protein intake throughout the day, and the presence of other nutrients.

Additionally, excess amino acids that are not immediately used for muscle protein synthesis can be used for other metabolic purposes, such as energy production or the synthesis of other necessary compounds in the body.

Therefore, the body has efficient mechanisms for handling and using ingested protein, even in amounts exceeding 30 grams per meal.

74

**The absorption of nutrients by the body
is a highly efficient process.**

It is estimated that approximately 95% of the ingested nutrients are absorbed, while the remaining 5% is used by the gut flora or expelled with the feces.

This high level of efficiency ensures that the body obtains most of the essential nutrients needed for its functioning.

Nutrient absorption occurs primarily in the small intestine.

During digestion, macronutrients (carbohydrates, proteins, and fats) and micronutrients (vitamins and minerals) are broken down into their basic components.

Carbohydrates are converted into simple sugars, proteins into amino acids, and fats into fatty acids and glycerol.

These basic components are absorbed through the walls of the small intestine and transported into the bloodstream for distribution and use throughout the body.

The efficiency of absorption does not vary significantly with meal frequency.

Studies have shown that there are no significant differences in hormones related to the availability of carbohydrates and fats, such as insulin and adiponectin, when comparing the intake of one meal a day to the intake of three meals a day.

This suggests that the body can effectively handle and distribute nutrients regardless of meal frequency, as long as the total daily intake of nutrients is adequate.

Insulin is a crucial hormone in regulating blood glucose levels.

Its primary function is to facilitate the absorption of glucose by the body's cells for use as energy or for storage as glycogen in the liver and muscles.

Adiponectin, on the other hand, is a hormone that plays a role in regulating the metabolism of glucose and fatty acids, enhancing insulin sensitivity, and reducing inflammation.

The gut flora, or intestinal microbiota, also plays an important role in the absorption and utilization of nutrients.

These bacteria ferment indigestible dietary fibers, producing short-chain fatty acids (SCFAs) like butyrate, which can be used as an energy source by the cells of the colon.

Additionally, the intestinal microbiota helps synthesize certain vitamins, such as vitamin K and some B vitamins, and facilitates the absorption of minerals like calcium and magnesium.

It is important to note that while nutrient absorption is generally efficient, it can be affected by various factors, including the health of the gastrointestinal tract, diet composition, and the presence of certain absorption inhibitors.

For example, the presence of phytates in certain grains and legumes can reduce the absorption of minerals such as iron and zinc.

Furthermore, medical conditions like celiac disease, inflammatory bowel disease, and gastrointestinal infections can compromise nutrient absorption.

75

The absorption of amino acids is a complex and efficient process that occurs primarily in the small intestine.

Amino acids, the building blocks of proteins, are absorbed by the intestinal cells (enterocytes) after the digestion of proteins in the gastrointestinal tract.

This process is essential for the maintenance and repair of tissues, the synthesis of new proteins, and the supply of energy.

When amino acids are absorbed, around 30-50% are retained in the intestinal cells, which have a particular preference for two amino acids: glutamine and aspartate (the form in which aspartic acid can be found).

These amino acids play crucial roles in intestinal function and health.

For example, glutamine is an important energy source for enterocytes and is essential for the integrity and maintenance of the intestinal barrier.

Aspartate is also used in various metabolic pathways within the intestinal cells.

In situations where protein or glucose intake is low, intestinal cells can release amino acids to be used by the body, thereby preventing the degradation of muscle mass.

This demonstrates the intestine's capacity to act as a reservoir of amino acids and its role in regulating protein metabolism.

The release of amino acids by the intestinal cells is a strategy of the body to maintain protein balance and provide necessary nutrients during periods of nutritional deficit.

The process of amino acid absorption can be affected by the saturation of transporters.

When protein intake is very high, the amino acid transporters in the intestinal cells can become saturated, limiting the amount of amino acids that can be absorbed at any given time.

As a result, more amino acids may reach the colon, where they can be fermented by the gut microbiota, producing various metabolites, some of which can be beneficial, while others may not be.

For individuals with damaged intestinal mucosa, such as those with inflammatory bowel diseases or irritable bowel syndrome, amino acid absorption can be even more problematic.

In such cases, a high protein intake in a single meal may not be ideal, as the absorption capacity is compromised.

Distributing protein intake throughout the day in several meals may be more beneficial to optimize amino acid absorption and reduce the burden on the intestine.

Maintaining a healthy intestinal mucosa is crucial for protein metabolism and efficient amino acid absorption.

The integrity of the intestinal mucosa ensures that amino acids are properly absorbed and that the intestine can perform its role as a protective barrier and metabolically active organ.

The utilization of protein in the body depends on several factors, including the quality of the protein and the type of protein consumed.

Protein quality determines the efficiency with which amino acids are retained and used for protein synthesis, while the type of protein influences the rate at which amino acids are released into the bloodstream and used by the body.

Protein quality refers to its essential amino acid composition and bioavailability.

High-quality proteins, such as whey and casein, contain all the essential amino acids in adequate proportions to support protein synthesis.

On the other hand, some plant proteins, such as soy protein, may have limitations in certain essential amino acids and lower bioavailability.

When comparing high-quality proteins like whey with plant proteins, it is observed that whey tends to increase protein synthesis more effectively and reduces urea production, indicating better amino acid utilization.

The type of protein also plays a crucial role in amino acid utilization.

Fast proteins, such as whey, are digested and absorbed quickly, resulting in a rapid increase in amino acid levels in the bloodstream.

This can be beneficial for post-workout protein synthesis, where a rapid availability of amino acids is required for muscle repair and growth.

In contrast, slow proteins, such as casein, are digested and absorbed more slowly, releasing amino acids over an extended period and maintaining a positive nitrogen balance for a longer time.

This can be beneficial for sustaining protein synthesis and reducing protein degradation during fasting periods or between meals.

The choice between fast and slow proteins may depend on the individual's specific needs and their eating pattern.

For those who consume protein in multiple meals throughout the day, the difference in absorption speed may be less significant, as amino acid levels remain consistently elevated.

However, for older individuals or those practicing intermittent fasting, consuming slow proteins like casein may be more beneficial for maintaining protein synthesis and reducing muscle catabolism during longer periods without food intake.

77

Body fat percentage and health are closely related, and maintaining a healthy level of body fat is crucial for overall well-being.

However, it is important to differentiate between extremely low levels of body fat and healthy levels that promote good health.

An extremely low body fat percentage, such as less than 6-8% in men or less than 12% in women, can have adverse health effects.

These low levels, typical of competitive bodybuilders or individuals with eating disorders like anorexia, can compromise immune function, disrupt hormonal balance, and negatively affect reproductive function and bone health.

On the other hand, maintaining a body fat percentage within a healthy range is associated with numerous health benefits.

A healthy level of body fat allows for optimal hormonal function, protects vital organs, and provides an energy reserve.

Generally, a healthy body fat range is approximately 10-20% for men and 20-30% for women, although these ranges can vary depending on age and other individual factors.

Overweight and obesity, defined by body fat percentages above the recommended levels, are linked to a higher risk of developing a range of chronic health problems, including cardiovascular diseases, type 2 diabetes, hypertension, certain types of cancer, and joint diseases.

In countries like Spain, more than half of the population is overweight or obese, highlighting the importance of addressing and managing excess body fat to improve public health.

Besides health risks, excess body fat can negatively impact quality of life and emotional well-being.

It can affect mobility, self-esteem, and body image, and increase the risk of developing mood disorders such as depression and anxiety.

On the other hand, the interest in reducing body fat percentage is often motivated by aesthetic reasons rather than health.

The culture of body image and the pressure to achieve certain aesthetic standards can lead to unhealthy behaviors, such as extreme diets and excessive exercise.

It is crucial to find a balance that prioritizes health while pursuing reasonable and sustainable aesthetic goals.

Maintaining a healthy body fat percentage involves a combination of healthy lifestyle habits, including a balanced, nutrient-rich diet, regular exercise, and adequate rest.

A balanced diet should include a variety of foods that provide the necessary vitamins, minerals, and macronutrients for optimal body function.

Regular exercise, including both aerobic and resistance activities, helps maintain energy balance and develop muscle mass, contributing to a healthy body composition.

78

The idea of losing localized fat through targeted exercises is a widely spread but generally debunked myth.

The theory behind this idea is that by exercising certain muscle groups, fat loss will be stimulated in that specific area, resulting in a more toned and defined appearance.

This belief is particularly popular in the context of abdominal fat loss through exercises like sit-ups and crunches.

However, numerous studies have shown that fat loss cannot be targeted in this way.

Instead, fat loss occurs systemically, that is, throughout the entire body, and is mainly influenced by genetic, hormonal, and lifestyle factors.

For example, a study conducted by Ramírez-Campillo et al. in 2013 found that a training protocol focusing exclusively on the legs did not result in significant fat loss in the legs, but rather in other areas of the body such as the abdominal region and arms.

Another study with tennis players showed that although the dominant (trained) arm had greater muscle circumference compared to the non-dominant arm, the skinfold fat measurements were similar in both arms, suggesting that localized exercise does not specifically reduce fat in that area.

While most studies conclude that localized fat loss is a myth, recent research suggests that certain methods might influence the distribution of fat loss.

A study published by Scotto di Palumbo et al. in 2017 found that combining strength training with aerobic exercises could enhance fat burning in the areas stimulated by strength training.

In this study, one group of participants performed strength training on their upper limbs followed by aerobic exercises with their lower limbs, while another group did the opposite.

The results showed that although overall fat loss was similar in both groups, the reduction of fat in the specific areas worked on with strength training was more pronounced.

These findings suggest that there might be a small localized fat loss effect due to increased blood flow and lipolysis in the subcutaneous fat tissue near the muscles that were intensely exercised.

However, these effects are relatively modest and do not represent a definitive solution for localized fat loss.

It is important to note that these studies were conducted on specific population groups, such as untrained women with normal weight or overweight, so the results should not be extrapolated to all individuals.

Moreover, the effects observed in these studies are minor compared to the overall fat loss achieved through a balanced approach of diet and exercise.

79

The myth that you should not eat carbohydrates or fruit at night because they cause weight gain is false and has been debunked by numerous studies in the field of nutrition.

This myth holds that consuming carbohydrates at dinner, since you go to sleep shortly afterward, will turn them into fat.

However, this belief does not have a solid scientific basis.

In reality, carbohydrates are not particularly efficient at converting into fat in the body.

For carbohydrates to be transformed into fat, approximately 23% of the ingested calories are needed in the conversion process, whereas fats require only about 3% of the ingested energy to be stored as fat.

This process is known as de novo lipogenesis and is relatively inefficient in humans when consuming a balanced diet.

When carbohydrates are consumed, they are primarily stored as glycogen in muscle tissue and the liver.

They will only convert into fat if consumed in excess, meaning when ingested calories significantly exceed expended calories.

The caloric surplus required for carbohydrates to convert into fat is considerably high, around 700 kcal above daily caloric expenditure.

This same principle applies to proteins and fats: any caloric excess, regardless of the source, can result in fat storage.

Therefore, if your daily carbohydrate intake should be 300 grams and by dinner you have consumed 220 grams, you can consume the remaining 80 grams without any issues.

What matters is the total caloric balance and the distribution of macronutrients throughout the day, not the specific timing of food consumption.

To determine how many carbohydrates you should consume daily, you can multiply your daily caloric needs by 0.5 (assuming that 50% of your calories should come from carbohydrates) and then divide that result by 4, since each gram of carbohydrates provides 4 kcal.

For example, in a diet of 2500 kcal per day:

- 50% of 2500 kcal = 1250 kcal from carbohydrates.

- 1250 kcal / 4 kcal per gram = 313 grams of carbohydrates per day.

80

The belief that creatine is responsible for water retention is false.

Creatine is a compound naturally found in our muscles and plays a crucial role in the regeneration of ATP, which is the main energy source for muscle contractions during high-intensity exercise.

Its specific function is to donate a phosphate group to ADP (adenosine diphosphate) to regenerate ATP (adenosine triphosphate), thus allowing the continuation of intense muscular activity.

The water retention associated with creatine supplementation is primarily due to the relationship between glycogen and water in the muscles.

Glycogen, the stored form of carbohydrates in the body, retains a significant amount of water.

Specifically, each gram of glycogen stored in the muscles is associated with approximately three grams of water.

When creatine is taken as a supplement, one of its effects is to increase the amount of phosphocreatine in the muscles, which in turn can increase the muscle's capacity to store glycogen.

This increase in glycogen storage leads to greater water retention within the muscle.

However, this water retention is intracellular, meaning it occurs within the muscle cells, and not extracellular, which is commonly perceived as "water retention."

The intracellular water retention due to increased glycogen can make the muscles appear fuller and more voluminous, but this is not the same as subcutaneous water retention, which can cause a bloated or swollen appearance.

Therefore, the perception that creatine causes water retention is a misunderstanding.

What actually happens is an increase in muscle volume due to greater hydration of the muscle cells.

Moreover, this effect is reversible and temporary.

When glycogen stores are depleted, such as during prolonged exercise or when carbohydrate intake is reduced, the associated water is also lost, and intracellular hydration levels return to normal.

81

The idea that the "anabolic window" only lasts 30 minutes after exercise is a widely spread myth in the world of fitness and nutrition.

This concept holds that there is a short period immediately after training during which the consumption of protein and nutrients is crucial to maximize muscle protein synthesis and promote muscle growth.

However, scientific evidence suggests that this anabolic window is not as strict or limited as previously believed.

Research, such as that by Tipton and colleagues, has shown that the ingestion of essential amino acids or protein before training can elevate plasma amino acid levels for up to two hours after completing exercise.

This indicates that amino acids remain available for muscle protein synthesis for an extended period, not just during the first 30 minutes post-exercise.

Additionally, other studies have shown that muscle protein synthesis can be elevated for several hours after exercise, and in some cases, up to 24 hours.

Therefore, the need to consume protein immediately after training is not as critical as it has been promoted.

The most important thing is to ensure an adequate protein intake throughout the day to support recovery and muscle growth.

The concern that not consuming a protein shake immediately after exercise will lead to a catabolic state (muscle breakdown) is unfounded.

If an adequate amount of protein has already been consumed before training, plasma amino acid levels will remain sufficient to promote protein synthesis and prevent muscle catabolism.

Furthermore, studies have shown that the most important factor for muscle gain is the total daily protein intake, not necessarily the exact timing of consumption.

As long as the recommended amounts of protein are consumed throughout the day, the benefits for muscle growth and recovery will be optimal.

82

The myth that bread makes you gain weight is false.

What really contributes to weight gain is consuming more calories than are expended, generally due to excessive caloric intake without adequate compensation through physical exercise.

Bread, like other starchy foods (cereals, pasta), is an important source of carbohydrates, which are essential nutrients for providing energy to the body.

The carbohydrates in bread play a crucial role in protein sparing.

If carbohydrate intake is insufficient, the body will begin to use proteins as an energy source, instead of allowing them to fulfill their primary function of building and repairing tissues.

Therefore, including carbohydrates in the diet is vital for balanced nutrition and to ensure that proteins can perform their proper functions.

Bread is not inherently harmful or fattening by itself.

The issue lies more with the foods that are often paired with bread, such as jams, butter, sauces, and cold cuts, which can add a significant amount of extra calories to the daily diet.

These accompaniments, more than the bread itself, can contribute to caloric excess and, consequently, weight gain.

Additionally, it is important to consider the type of bread consumed.

Whole grain breads, for example, have a higher fiber content than refined white breads, which can help increase satiety and control appetite, thereby aiding in maintaining a healthy weight.

83

The myth that all foods with a high glycemic index (GI) should be avoided is false and oversimplifies the complexity of nutrition.

The glycemic index is a value that indicates the rate at which a specific carbohydrate increases blood glucose levels, with pure glucose serving as the reference point with a GI value of 100.

In theory, the higher the GI, the more rapidly blood sugar levels rise.

However, in practice, the usefulness of the GI is limited for several reasons.

First, the glycemic index of a food can change significantly when consumed with other foods.

When a plate contains a mix of fats, proteins, or high-fiber foods, the GI of the food can be completely altered.

For example, if you consume white rice (GI of 70) with broccoli (high in fiber) and chicken (high in protein and leucine), the GI of the white rice can be reduced to levels similar to brown rice.

Additionally, there are instances of foods with a high GI that actually contain very little sugar.

Watermelon is a good example, with a GI of 75, but it is mainly composed of water, fiber, and a small amount of sugar.

Comparing this with foods like sugary ice cream or mayonnaise, which have a lower GI (around 60) but contain much more sugar and fat, illustrates the absurdity of basing dietary decisions solely on the GI.

Another significant limitation of the GI is that this index is based on foods consumed in isolation, without accompanying other foods.

In real life, foods are rarely eaten alone.

The combination of foods, such as fats, proteins, and fiber, can significantly alter the body's glycemic response, making the GI of a specific food less relevant.

The GI also ignores the glycemic load (GL), which considers both the quality (GI) and the quantity of carbohydrates in a portion of food.

The glycemic load is a more accurate measure of how a food will affect blood glucose levels.

For example, a small portion of a high-GI food can have a low glycemic load and therefore a minimal impact on blood sugar levels.

84

Foods labeled as "light" are not necessarily healthy or suitable for consumption at all times.

The term "light" is used to describe products that have a lower concentration of fat, sugar, or calories than their original versions.

However, this label can be misleading and does not always mean that the food is a healthy option.

Originally, "light" foods were those with a lower fat concentration compared to their regular counterparts.

However, today there is a wide variety of "light" and "fitness" products, which has led to confusion about what being "light" really means.

"Light" foods can be divided into two main categories: those that do not contain sugar and those that do not contain fat.

For "light" foods that do not contain sugar, large amounts of trans and saturated fats are often added to compensate for the loss of flavor and texture provided by sugar.

Trans and saturated fats, especially in large quantities, can be harmful to health, increasing the risk of cardiovascular diseases and other health problems.

On the other hand, "light" foods that do not contain fat often have added syrups and glucose and fructose syrups to maintain a pleasant taste.

These added sugars can contribute to weight gain, poor blood glucose control, and the risk of developing type 2 diabetes, among other health issues.

The food industry uses these techniques to ensure that "light" products remain attractive and tasty to consumers.

However, this often comes at the expense of the nutritional health of the product.

Therefore, it is important not to be swayed by the "light" label and instead carefully review the ingredient list and nutritional information.

It is essential to avoid overconsumption of "light" foods and to be aware of their ingredients.

Consuming these products in excess can lead to a high intake of unhealthy ingredients, such as trans fats, saturated fats, and added sugars.

Rather than relying solely on foods labeled as "light," it is better to focus on a balanced diet that includes fresh and minimally processed foods, such as fruits, vegetables, whole grains, lean proteins, and healthy fats.

85

The idea that cheat meals have no physiological effects is false.

While it is true that a cheat meal can provide significant psychological benefits, such as reducing stress and the monotony of a restrictive diet, it also has important physiological effects on the body.

When a cheat meal is consumed, for example, a pizza, there is an increase in the levels of thyroid hormones T3 and T4.

These hormones are closely related to the regulation of metabolism.

An increase in T3 and T4 levels can temporarily boost the metabolic rate, helping the body burn more calories.

Additionally, a cheat meal can also increase the concentration of leptin, a hormone produced by fat cells that is related to the regulation of appetite and satiety.

An increase in leptin levels can enhance the feeling of fullness and reduce hunger, which can be beneficial for long-term weight control.

A cheat meal can also improve carbohydrate metabolism and the transport of glucose to the muscles.

This is particularly relevant after a period of calorie-restricted dieting, where muscle glycogen levels may be low.

A high-carbohydrate meal can replenish glycogen stores and improve the body's ability to handle glucose.

From an evolutionary perspective, the human body is designed to respond to fluctuations in caloric intake.

During prolonged periods of caloric restriction, basal metabolism tends to decrease as a mechanism for conserving energy.

This phenomenon is known as "metabolic adaptation" or "adaptive thermogenesis."

A cheat meal can help mitigate this effect by providing a temporary increase in caloric intake, which can "reset" the metabolism and prevent an excessive decrease in metabolic rate.

This temporary increase in metabolism and hormone levels related to the cheat meal is known as the "set point" effect.

The body adjusts its metabolic rate in response to variations in caloric intake, and a cheat meal can help maintain this balance.

86

The myth that high egg consumption should be avoided because it raises cholesterol is false.

This misunderstanding can be quickly resolved by understanding that dietary cholesterol does not significantly impact blood cholesterol levels for most people.

The main reason lies in the functioning of the liver, which acts as the primary regulator of cholesterol in the body.

The liver has the ability to synthesize cholesterol.

When dietary cholesterol intake is high, the liver reduces endogenous cholesterol production to balance the levels.

Conversely, when dietary cholesterol intake is low, the liver increases production to ensure the body has enough to carry out its essential functions.

This regulatory mechanism means that the body can adapt to variations in dietary cholesterol intake.

Numerous studies have shown that for most people, consuming cholesterol-rich foods, such as eggs, does not significantly impact blood cholesterol levels.

In fact, eggs are a nutrient-rich source, providing high-quality proteins, vitamins, minerals, and important antioxidants such as lutein and zeaxanthin, which are beneficial for eye health.

It is important to note that although egg consumption is generally safe and healthy, some people may be hypersensitive to dietary cholesterol.

These individuals, known as "hyper-responders," may experience a more significant increase in blood cholesterol levels in response to dietary cholesterol.

However, even in these cases, the impact on LDL (bad cholesterol) and HDL (good cholesterol) levels may not be clinically significant and should be evaluated individually.

Moreover, the effects of dietary cholesterol on blood cholesterol levels are less concerning than the effects of saturated and trans fats.

These fats, found in many processed foods and some animal fats, have a much more significant impact on LDL cholesterol levels and the risk of cardiovascular diseases.

87

The myth that mixing carbohydrates with proteins leads to weight gain is false and has no scientific basis.

Dissociated diets, which are based on not mixing carbohydrate-rich foods (such as cereals, pasta, potatoes, bread) with protein foods (such as meat, fish, eggs) in the same meal, rely on the erroneous belief that weight gain is due to poor digestion resulting from an incorrect combination of foods.

The reality is that our bodies are perfectly equipped with enzymes capable of digesting carbohydrates and proteins simultaneously without reducing their activity or efficiency.

The human digestive system is highly adaptable and efficient at digesting a variety of mixed foods in a single meal.

Specific digestive enzymes, such as amylases for carbohydrates and proteases for proteins, work in coordination to break down nutrients and allow their effective absorption.

The idea that combining carbohydrates and proteins in a single meal can cause weight gain due to poor digestion lacks scientific evidence.

In fact, many healthy and balanced meals contain a mix of carbohydrates, proteins, and fats, providing a range of essential nutrients needed for a balanced diet and optimal health.

The reason why some people may lose weight on dissociated diets is not due to the separation of macronutrients, but rather to the monotony and restriction these diets impose.

By severely limiting food combinations, these diets can become boring and less appealing, which may lead to an overall reduction in caloric intake simply because people tend to eat less.

Printed in Great Britain
by Amazon